TURNED BOXES

TURNED BOXES

40 INSPIRING BOXES BY EXPERT MAKERS

First published 2017 by
Guild of Master Craftsman Publications Ltd
Castle Place, 166 High Street, Lewes,
East Sussex, BN7 1XU, UK

ISBN 978 1 78494 248 9

Publisher Jonathan Bailey
Production Manager Jim Bulley
Senior Project Editor Wendy McAngus
Editor Stephen Haynes
Managing Art Editor Gilda Pacitti
Designer Luana Gobbo
Contributors Nick Arnull, Mark Baker, Bob Chapman, Sue Harker, Dennis Keeling, Mike Mahoney, Tracy Owen, Andrew Potocnik, Mark Sanger, Neil Scobie, Jo Winter
Technical Consultant Alan Goodsell

Photography Step-by-step photographs by the project authors; styled shots by Anthony Bailey
Illustrations Simon Rodway

Colour origination by GMC Reprographics
Printed and bound in Malaysia

A NOTE ON MEASUREMENTS
Though every attempt has been made to ensure that the metric and imperial measurements are sufficiently accurate for practical purposes, some rounding up or down has been inevitable. When following the projects, use either the metric or the imperial units – do not mix the two. If in doubt, make a full-size working drawing before you start cutting.

CONTENTS

INTRODUCTION

There are few items of woodwork more appealing than the small turned box. Compact enough to hold in the hand and inspect at close quarters, it offers the perfect showcase for the maker's technical skill and artistic taste. The articles brought together in this book, by eminent makers from around the world, afford an excellent introduction to this absorbing art.

Practice makes perfect, and the book begins with a generous selection of basic boxes to help you build and develop your foundation skills. Learn the difference between endgrain and crossgrain turning, and how to ensure an accurately fitting lid – one of the hallmarks of a well-made box.

Finial boxes are a popular form today, and we include a selection of boxes with handles or finials of many different kinds. Other designs explore the use of colour, either by juxtaposing different wood species or by adding colour to the finished product. One particularly colourful project is not even made of wood. There are designs that feature simple carving, and the cutting and reassembling of turned components. There is bound to be something here to inspire any turner.

Step-by-step photographs allow you to look over the designer-maker's shoulder as the work takes shape. Each project includes a full list of tools and materials required, so you can make sure before you start work that you have what you need. Measured drawings, including cross sections, show all the details you need to know, whether you plan to copy the projects closely or use them as a springboard for your own original ideas.

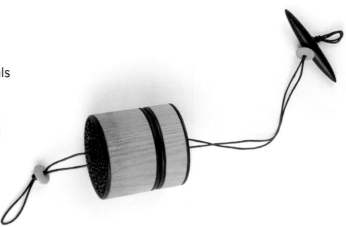

ENDGRAIN BOXES

Although box making offers endless possibilities, there are only two main types to turn: those with solid lids, and those with hollowed lids. Here Mark Sanger turns two boxes using fully seasoned endgrain blanks – that is, with the wood mounted so that its grain runs in line with the spindle axis of the lathe.

WHAT YOU NEED

- Endgrain blanks in spalted European sycamore (*Acer pseudoplatanus*):
  Solid lid: 2¾ × 2¾ × 3⅛in (70 × 70 × 80mm)
  Hollowed lid: 3⅜ × 3⅜ × 4in (85 × 85 × 100mm)
- 1in (25mm) spindle roughing gouge
- ⅜in (10mm) spindle gouge with fingernail grind
- ½in (12mm) skew chisel
- 1in (25mm) round-nose scraper
- ¼in (6mm) parting tool
- ¹⁄₁₆in (2mm) parting tool
- Fine-blade saw
- Abrasive, 120–400 grit

- Small sanding arbor in jam chuck
- Home-made bent wire sanding arbor
- Pencil
- Rule
- Callipers
- Cellulose sanding sealer
- Kitchen towel
- Buffing system
- Microcrystalline wax
- PPE: latex gloves, face mask, respirator/dust mask, extraction

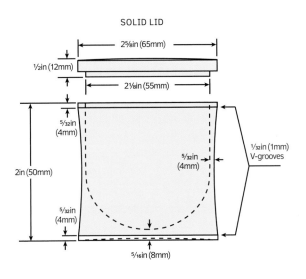

SOLID LID

2⅝in (65mm)

½in (12mm)

2⅛in (55mm)

5⁄32in (4mm)

5⁄32in (4mm)

1⁄32in (1mm) V-grooves

2in (50mm)

5⁄32in (4mm)

5⁄16in (8mm)

HOLLOWED LID

19⁄32in (15mm)

⅜in (10mm)

7⁄32in (5mm)

1¾in (45mm) Ø

1 11⁄16in (43mm) Ø

1⅛in (28mm)

5⁄32in (4mm)

1⅜in (35mm) Ø

5⁄32in (4mm) Ø

3¼in (85mm)

3⅛in (80mm) Ø

1⁄16in (1.5mm)

1⅛in (30mm)

INTRODUCTION

Offcuts of exotic or expensive timbers that are too small for other projects are an excellent source of wood for box making, but there are also many synthetic materials available that are ideal, such as acrylic or resin, faux ivory, horn and tortoiseshell.

Most box designs can be made using a basic beginner's set of gouges and scrapers. Dedicated tools such as screw-threading tools and cranked scrapers are not used here, but as you become more skilled you may wish to investigate these.

WOOD SELECTION

Any sound timber can be turned, although close-grained and dense timbers such as yew (*Taxus* spp.), beech (*Fagus* spp.) and fruitwoods are most suited as these take fine detail with good strength. For these projects, fully seasoned wood is used; for this we have two options: to include the pith, as with branch wood, or to use a processed blank with the pith excluded, as in the diagram below.

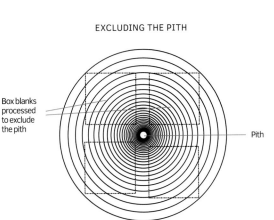

EXCLUDING THE PITH

Box blanks processed to exclude the pith

Pith

A blank without pith is a more stable option for box making and is often preferred. If you do decide to use branch wood, it must be fully seasoned, or there is a high risk of cracking from the pith outwards. No matter how well seasoned wood is, there will still be a very small amount of movement after turning, due to the internal tensions being released. This movement, while minimal, can be felt in a box by the fit of the lid, which tightens in two places as it is twisted in the box one full rotation. For this reason, boxes turned to finished size in one go, like the first project here, will suit a looser-fitting lid, which is typically seen in the design of tea, coffee and sugar caddies, to name a few. If a stable, snug lid is required, then the box is first rough-turned from a seasoned blank and allowed to settle for several days before turning to completion, as shown in the second project.

THE PERFECT FIT

A snug-fitting lid that 'pops' when removed is often viewed by woodturners as the correct fit for a box. However, the correct fit is one that suits its intended use. A pill box, for instance, should have a tight-fitting lid that will not fall off when carried in a pocket or bag, while an earring box suits a free-fitting lid that can be removed and replaced with one hand, leaving the other free to remove and replace earrings.

CUTTING WITH THE GRAIN

Cutting with the grain is essential for efficient wood removal and for achieving a good finish from the tool. The outside of an endgrain project is turned from outside to centre, while hollowing is achieved by cutting from the centre out (see diagram on page 10).

CUTTING SEQUENCE FOR SOLID-LID BOX

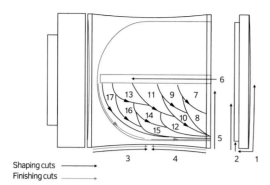

Shaping cuts ———→
Finishing cuts ·········→

DRILLING AND HOLLOWING OUT

Use a spindle gouge that has a fingernail grind; to drill out, set the toolrest so the gouge cuts on centre, with the tool's shaft and flute horizontal. Mark the depth on the gouge shaft and drill out, withdrawing regularly to clear shavings. To hollow, present the spindle gouge to cut on centre with the shaft trailing slightly downwards. The gouge edge is presented to cut at 10 o'clock, with the tool shaft rotated anticlockwise 10–20° so the cutting forces are supported by the toolrest. The cut is made from the inside out, using the intersection of the tool shaft and toolrest as a fulcrum.

DRILLING OUT

HOLLOWING OUT

MAKING A BOX WITH SOLID LID

1 Mark the centre at both ends of the blank and mount between centres. Rough out the blank to a cylinder using a spindle roughing gouge and produce a spigot at one end to suit your chuck jaws, then remove and tighten into the chuck. Refine the outside and clean up the front face using a ½in (12mm) skew chisel or a ⅜in (10mm) spindle gouge.

2 Using a pencil and rule, mark a line on the outside ⅜in (10mm) down from the top, and a second line for the base of the box. With a ¼in (6mm) parting tool, part in to the left of the first line to a depth of ⁵⁄₁₆in (8mm) to produce a spigot that will fit inside the finished box, making sure it is parallel.

3 Use the toe of a ½in (12mm) skew chisel to produce two small V-grooves ⁵⁄₃₂in (4mm) down from the rim and ⁵⁄₃₂in (4mm) up from the baseline you have drawn.

4 Use a 1/16in (2mm) parting tool to part the lid off from the box, leaving a small piece of the spigot visible on the box. Alternatively, leaving 3/8in (10mm) of waste, stop the lathe and cut through the remaining part with a fine saw.

5 Drill to depth and hollow out as described above, using a 3/8in (10mm) spindle gouge. Open out until the lid fits tightly into the box and refine with a round-nose scraper. My scraper has been ground further around into the left edge to allow for scraping on the side of the box.

6 Finish the inside with abrasive from 120 to 400 grit, giving a loose fit for the lid to take into account any later movement in the wood. The abrasive is stuck to a small sanding arbor in a handle, making it easier to reach down into the base of the box.

7 Use the 1/16in (2mm) parting tool to part the box off from the waste at the marked line, just as you did with the lid. Angle the tool slightly up into the base to produce a concave surface so it will sit without rocking.

8 Finish the base and the underside of the lid with abrasive attached to a sanding arbor, which is fitted into a waste piece of wood placed in the lathe chuck.

9 Apply sanding sealer to the box and lid, buff using a buffing system and compound, and apply microcrystalline wax to finish.

MAKING A BOX WITH HOLLOWED LID

1 Mark the centre at both ends of the blank and mount between centres. Rough to a cylinder and produce a spigot at each end to suit your chuck. Mark a line ¾in (20mm) down from the front face, then part to the left of this line with a ¼in (6mm) parting tool and callipers to produce a spigot 1⅜in (35mm) in diameter.

2 Rough down the profile for the lid and base, leaving a fraction oversize. Make sure you leave a shoulder at each spigot for mounting in the chuck.

3 Tighten the base spigot into the chuck and bring up the tail centre for light support. Using a 1⁄16in (2mm) parting tool, part into the spigot, leaving a registration on the base of the lid. Stop short of parting all the way through, then stop the lathe and cut through the remainder with a fine-blade saw. Hollow out the base and the internal profile of the lid with a ⅜in (10mm) spindle gouge, leaving both undersize.

4 Remove from the lathe and allow to settle for a few days in a domestic environment before proceeding. Alternatively, if you want a loose-fitting lid, continue as follows, taking into account any movement in the wood that may occur.

5 Once settled, mount the lid in the chuck. Measure the spigot of the box and subtract 1⁄16in (2mm), then mark this accurately on the front face. Refine the internal profile using a ⅜in (10mm) spindle gouge, stopping short of the marked line.

6 With the toe of a ½in (12mm) skew chisel held horizontally on the toolrest, produce a parallel-sided recess, just cutting away part of the drawn line.

7 Finish with abrasive from 180 to 400 grit, being careful not to alter the profile or size of the recess. Apply liquid cellulose sanding sealer, allow this to dry and then buff with safety cloth or kitchen towel with the lathe set to 1,000rpm. Remove from the chuck and make a jam chuck to suit the internal recess of the lid; jam the lid onto this, placing kitchen towel between to prevent marking the finished surface. Profile the top of the box to the final shape using a ⅜in (10mm) spindle gouge. Finish with abrasive as before, then remove.

8 Mount the base into the chuck and refine the diameter of the spigot, checking regularly with the lid until you have a tight fit. Remove and set to one side.

9 Refine the outside profile using a ⅜in (10mm) spindle gouge, leaving it thick at the base to allow for hollowing in the next step.

10 Measure the height of the base, subtract ¼in (6mm) and mark this onto the shaft of the gouge. Drill to depth and hollow to the final profile, checking the wall thickness with callipers as you progress. Remember the base is thicker than the final profile, so take this into account; refine the surface by taking a few fine finishing cuts.

11 Finish the inside and outside with abrasive by hand, from 120 to 320 grit. Here I am using a double length of stiff wire wrapped in duct tape, onto which hook-and-loop has been glued to hold the abrasive. This can be bent to the required profile for finishing the inside.

12 Reverse the base onto a jam chuck, bringing up the tail centre for support. Refine the base using a ⅜in (10mm) spindle gouge down into the foot; concave the underside of the foot so it will be stable in use, stopping a safe distance from the tail centre. Finish with abrasive by hand as before. Stop the lathe and cut through the remaining waste with a fine-bladed saw, refine with a sharp chisel or power carver and finish with abrasive by hand.

13 Apply cellulose sanding sealer to the outside of the base and lid, buff with your preferred buffing system, apply microcrystalline wax and finally buff with a soft cloth.

CROSSGRAIN BOX

Crossgrain turning – where the grain of the wood lies at right angles to the lathe axis – is an excellent choice for large boxes, because you can use commercially available bowl-turning blanks, which can often be found in quite large sizes. Here Mark Sanger looks at techniques to turn a crossgrain box from a seasoned European sycamore (*Acer pseudoplatanus*) bowl blank.

WHAT YOU NEED

- European sycamore, 6in (150mm) diameter × 4in (100mm) thick seasoned crossgrain blank
- Sycamore offcut, 1½ × 1½ × 2⅜in (40 × 40 × 60mm), for bead
- ⅜in (10mm) bowl gouge with fingernail or long grind
- ½in (12mm) skew chisel
- 1in (25mm) square-end scraper
- 1in (25mm) round-nose scraper
- ¼in (6mm) spindle gouge with fingernail grind
- ¼in (6mm) parting tool
- ¹⁄₁₆in (2mm) parting tool
- ¼in (6mm) point tool

- Fine-blade saw
- Abrasives, 120–400 grit
- ¼in (6mm) diameter twist drill and Jacobs chuck
- Small sanding arbor in jam chuck
- Pencil
- Rule
- Callipers and Vernier callipers
- Cellulose sanding sealer
- Kitchen towel
- Buffing system
- Microcrystalline wax
- PPE: latex gloves, face mask, respirator/dust mask, extraction

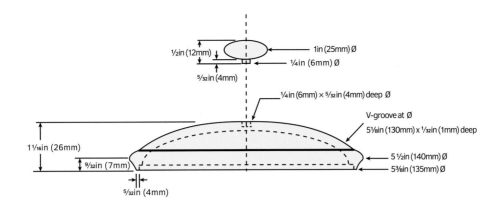

½in (12mm)

1in (25mm) Ø

¼in (6mm) Ø

5/32in (4mm)

¼in (6mm) × 5/32in (4mm) deep Ø

V-groove at Ø
5⅛in (130mm) x ¹⁄₃₂in (1mm) deep

1¹⁄₁₆in (26mm)

9/32in (7mm)

5 ½in (140mm) Ø
5⅜in (135mm) Ø

5/32in (4mm)

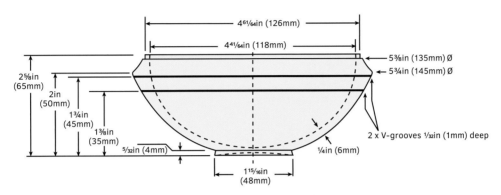

4⁶¹⁄₆₄in (126mm)

4⁴¹⁄₆₄in (118mm)

5⅜in (135mm) Ø
5¾in (145mm) Ø

2⅝in (65mm)

2in (50mm)

1¾in (45mm)

1⅜in (35mm)

5/32in (4mm)

2 x V-grooves ¹⁄₃₂in (1mm) deep

¼in (6mm)

1¹⁵⁄₁₆in (48mm)

INTRODUCTION

Seasoned endgrain or spindle blanks suitable for box making are generally available commercially only in sections up to 4in (100mm) square. Seasoned crossgrain bowl blanks, on the other hand, allow you to produce boxes and other lidded projects on a much larger scale. Seasoned European sycamore is used here, but any sound wood can be used. However, if your box design includes fine detail, then a close-grained dense timber is best suited, such as yew (*Taxus* spp.), beech (*Fagus* spp.) or fruitwoods. Try out the box described in this project or change the design to suit your own tastes.

CUTTING WITH THE GRAIN

Cutting with the grain is important for efficient wood removal, and to achieve a good finish from the tool. A crossgrain blank is cut in the opposite direction to that of endgrain wood: the outside profile is turned from the smallest diameter outwards, while the inside is hollowed from large diameter to small, as in the cutting sequence diagram.

DIRECTION OF CUTS
OR BOX AND LID

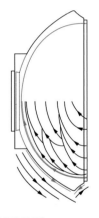

SHAPING CUTS ———→
FINISHING CUTS ———→

1 Mark the centre at both ends of the blank and mount between centres. Rough to the round with a ⅜in (10mm) bowl gouge, produce a spigot at each end to suit the jaws of your chuck, remove and tighten one end into the chuck.

2 Mark a line on the outside, one-third up from the left end. Use a ¼in (6mm) parting tool to part in to the right of this line to a depth of ½in (12mm), to produce a spigot that will fit up into the lid of the box; make sure the sides of the spigot are parallel.

3 Using a ⅜in (10mm) bowl gouge, rough out the profile of the base, leaving it oversize, by cutting with the grain as indicated in the cutting sequence diagram. When you come to the concave edge that leads into the join with the lid, it is simpler to shape this profile by cutting against the grain; this will not produce the best surface finish, but we will clean it up later by cutting with the grain once the wood has settled. When cutting against the grain, take small cuts with a freshly sharpened tool to minimize tearout. If you prefer to take the box down to final size at this stage, leave a little extra on the curve leading to the join so you can refine this once the lid has been parted, as shown in step 11.

4 Remove the work from the lathe and mount the base spigot into the chuck, then use a ⅜in (10mm) bowl gouge to profile the lid down to the concave section previously produced at the lid join; again, leave this slightly oversize. Use a 1/16in (2mm) parting tool to part the lid from the base, leaving a small section of the spigot for registration on the underside of the lid. This will be needed if you are finishing the box in one go.

5 Stop the lathe before parting all the way through, and cut through the remaining waste using a fine-bladed saw.

6 Use the ⅜in (10mm) bowl gouge to hollow out the body of the box by cutting from the outside into the centre, leaving it slightly thicker than the intended finished profile.

7 Mount the lid into the chuck and hollow as you did the base, again leaving oversize. Stop around ½in (12mm) from the registration line left when it was parted from the base. Keep the two sections together and store indoors for several days to allow any movement to settle.

8 One it has settled, mount the lid into the chuck and clean up the inside profile of the lid, remembering to leave a few millimetres of extra thickness so you can clean up the outside profile later when the lid is jammed onto the base.

9 Now refine the surface with a 1in (25mm) round-nose scraper.

10 Using the bowl gouge, take a fine cut to clean up the front face, then measure the outside diameter of the spigot of the box with Vernier callipers, remembering that it may have moved and gone slightly oval. You need to double-check this measurement through 90° to find the smallest diameter, then subtract ¹⁄₁₆in (2mm) and accurately mark this measurement on the front face of the lid, using a pencil and the calliper or rule. Use the toe of a ½in (12mm) skew chisel, held horizontal on the toolrest, to cut a parallel spigot inside the lid, making several plunge cuts into the face of the blank until you have removed half of the marked line.

11 Use the ³⁄₈in (10mm) bowl gouge to clean up the curve that leads to the rim of the lid. Unlike when roughing out, here we cut from inside out, cutting with the grain. Aim to leave a rim thickness of around ⁵⁄₃₂in (4mm) as per the drawing.

12 Finish the inside, rim and curve with abrasive from 120 to 400 grit, being careful not to alter the profile or size of the recess. Apply liquid cellulose sanding sealer to the inside of the lid and buff with kitchen towel or safety cloth with the lathe at 1,000rpm.

13 Mount the body of the box into the chuck and with a ¼in (6mm) spindle gouge clean up the face of the spigot that will fit into the lid. Clean up the shoulder leading into the spigot and the spigot itself, checking the fit regularly with the lid until you have a tight fit. A spindle gouge is used here instead of a parting tool as it produces a finer slicing cut through the endgrain sections compared to the parting tool, especially on low-density timbers.

14 Finish the inside profile using the ³⁄₈in (10mm) bowl gouge, leaving the final thickness of the spigot around ⁵⁄₃₂in (4mm). Refine the curve leading into the join as in step 11, by cutting with the grain outwards to the shoulder. Offer up the lid to check that the curves of the base and lid meet up exactly at the join, refine as required, then finish with abrasive, apply sanding sealer and buff as before.

15 Jam the lid onto the base (with a layer of kitchen towel in between if the fit is too loose), bringing up the tail centre for support. Use a ⅜in (10mm) bowl gouge to refine the outside profile with several fine cuts.

16 Refine the surface if required with a 1in (25mm) square-end scraper.

17 The next step, using a ¼in (6mm) point tool, is to produce a groove on the top of the lid ⁵⁄₁₆in (8mm) in from the rim.

18 You can now remove the tail centre and refine the top profile of the form by cutting away the chucking spigot with the bowl gouge, working outwards towards the rim. You can further refine with the 1in (25mm) square-end scraper as before.

19 Drill a ¼in (6mm) diameter hole, ⁵⁄₃₂in (4mm) deep, into the top of the lid with a twist drill held in a Jacobs chuck in the tail centre.

20 Use a piece of plastic laminate to burn a line by pushing it into the base of the groove while applying moderate pressure, with the lathe set to 1,500rpm. Alternatively, if you are not comfortable doing this, then you can use a fine-tip permanent marker. Finish the lid with abrasive from 120 to 400 grit. Remove the lid from the lathe and, using 180–240 grit abrasive, gently refine the outside surface of the spigot, fitting it into the lid until you have a fine fit.

21 Make a jam chuck from waste wood to accept the spigot of the box body, then jam the body onto this. Refine the profile from the chucking spigot up to the rim, using the ⅜in (10mm) bowl gouge.

22 Refine the surface finish with a 1in (25mm) square-end scraper.

23 Use a ¼in (6mm) spindle gouge to refine the base profile, producing the foot as you remove the waste. Hollow the foot so the box will sit stable in use.

24 Use a ¼in (6mm) point tool to produce a groove at the join of the foot and base, another ⁵⁄₃₂in (4mm) from the shoulder or incurve to the join, and a third ⁵⁄₁₆in (8mm) down from this. Burn lines into these using the laminate, or use a fine permanent marker as before.

25 Rough down the bead blank to the round, produce a spigot at one end and fit this into the chuck. Clean up the front face with a ¼in (6mm) spindle gouge, then mark two lines on the outside with a pencil and rule, the first denoting the height of the bead and the second at the centre of the bead. Using a ¼in (6mm) parting tool, part in left of the first pencil line for the height of the bead; part in half the diameter of the blank, giving clearance for shaping the left side of the bead with the gouge. Turn the right side of the bead with the ¼in (6mm) spindle gouge and finish with 180–400 grit abrasive.

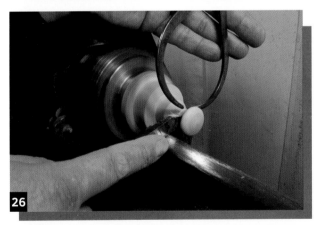

26 Continue profiling the left side of the bead with the spindle gouge, removing the waste as you progress deeper. Finish with abrasive as before and, with the ¼in (6mm) parting tool and callipers set to ¼in (6mm), part the spigot at the base of the bead to its finished size. Stop the lathe and cut through the spigot with a fine-blade saw, leaving the spigot ⁵⁄₃₂in (4mm) long to fit into the hole in the lid.

27 Apply sanding sealer to the outside of the box, lid and bead, allow to dry, then buff with your chosen buffing system and compound. Finally, apply several coats of microcrystalline wax by hand with a soft cloth and buff.

CURVED BOX

This project by Mark Sanger starts with unseasoned wood. This allows us to use sections that are too small for other projects, thus reducing waste and the cost of the wood we use. There is also a great satisfaction in making any project that follows a process all the way through from natural branch to finished item.

WHAT YOU NEED

- Unseasoned European sycamore (*Acer pseudoplatanus*) or other hardwood of your choice, 4in (100mm) long by 3in (75mm) diameter
- 1in (25mm) spindle roughing gouge
- ¼in (6mm) parting tool
- ¹⁄₁₆in (2mm) parting tool
- ½in (12mm) skew chisel
- ¼in (6mm) spindle gouge with fingernail profile
- ⅜in (10mm) spindle gouge with fingernail profile
- 1in (25mm) sawtooth bit

- Fine-blade saw
- Pencil
- Rule
- Callipers
- Abrasives 120–400 grit
- Cellulose sanding sealer
- Buffing system and compound
- Kitchen towel
- Microcrystalline wax
- PPE: face mask, respirator/dust mask, extraction

INTRODUCTION

Most species of wood can be used for box making; however, beginners should select pieces that do not have cracks or inclusions as, while these can add visual impact, they will cause you more problems than they are worth.

For this project the blank is processed and turned with the grain running in line with the spindle axis of the lathe. This orientation allows for strength, particularly across small sections, such as the spigot onto which the lid of the box fits.

The blank for this project has been processed to exclude the pith, as shown in the diagram below. This is because whole sections of branch wood have a high chance of cracking from the pith to the rim, while blanks excluding the pith can move out of shape during seasoning with less risk of failure. If sections of branch wood are used, they must be fully stable and seasoned or there is a high chance of failure, especially when the work is introduced to a warm, dry indoor environment.

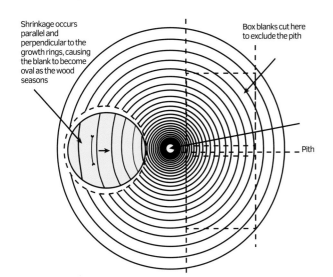

Shrinkage occurs parallel and perpendicular to the growth rings, causing the blank to become oval as the wood seasons

Box blanks cut here to exclude the pith

Pith

MAKING BOX BLANKS FROM UNSEASONED WOOD

Process blanks by cutting through your log or section so the grain runs through its length.

I make mine ½in (12mm) oversize to allow for cleaning up to size after the wood has seasoned. There are now two options: either (1) seal the blank using an emulsifying wax painted onto the end grain, or (2) rough-turn the box oversize, seal the end grain and tape the box and lid together. Write details of date, species and weight onto the blanks for reference. Weigh regularly over a few weeks, and once the weight has stabilized for a couple of weeks, take the item into your home to settle for a few more weeks, at which point the box can be finish-turned. Alternatively, if you are using already seasoned stock, rough out a few millimetres oversize, then take it into your home so the fibres can relax for a week prior to finish-turning.

If my blanks are cut from a freshly felled tree, I use method (1); if the wood is taken from planks or stock that has been cut for a few months, I go for method (2). Such wood rarely fails, as long as the rough blanks are stored in a cool, draught-free location.

TOOLS

Box making requires few tools. Here is a list of the ones I use most often; those used for this particular project are listed opposite.

- 1in (25mm) spindle roughing gouge
- ¼in (6mm) spindle gouge with fingernail profile
- ½in (12mm) skew chisel
- ¼in (6mm) parting tool
- ¹⁄₁₆in (2mm) parting tool
- Box scraper or standard ½in (12mm) round-nose or square-end scraper, depending upon internal box profile required

For boxes with a depth greater than 4in (100mm), and those whose shape consists of some form of curve – such as with an undercut hollow form – tools with beefed-up shafts and handles allow better control. For projects with an undercut body you may need a swan-neck tool, or one that has a swivelling tip arrangement. While there are many different tools for this purpose on the market, they all do one of two things: slice or scrape the wood fibres, as with standard turning tools. Many have interchangeable tips, thus making them useful for other projects and applications, with small tips for hollowing and larger tips for refining shapes. For small, simple boxes, the tools listed above will be fine.

DESIGNING A BOX FORM

The form or design of your box will depend on its intended use. If it is purely a utility box, then it must first and foremost serve this purpose well, such as allowing easy access for placing and removing items. It may, on the other hand, be intended purely for visual impact. In either case, we can produce a balanced form by using the 'rule of thirds'. This involves dividing the parts of our box into thirds, which adds balance and harmony to the finished box. In the diagram (right), you will see the profile of a standard utility box over which a grid of thirds has been laid. You can see that the join of the lid is located two-thirds of the way up from the base. It may be that the use of the box dictates the lid is positioned in a different place – such as a shallow pill box, which would suit having the join halfway up. The type of box does ultimately dictate where the base and lid join, but as a starting point, dividing the form into thirds is a good practice. Look around at boxes, perfume containers, etc. and see how they have been designed, taking into account the use and proportions.

USING THE RULE OF THIRDS

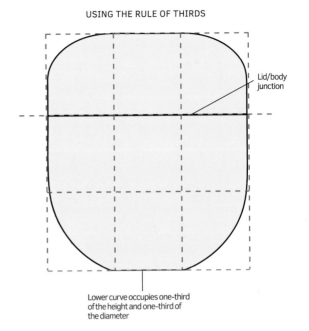

Lid/body junction

Lower curve occupies one-third of the height and one-third of the diameter

1 Mark centres at both ends of the blank and mount between centres. Using a spindle roughing gouge, rough to a cylinder, leaving slightly oversize. Use a ¼in (6mm) parting tool to clean up both ends to a safe distance from the drive and tail centres. Produce a spigot at each end to suit the jaws of your chuck, refining if needed with a ½in (12mm) skew chisel held horizontal on the toolrest in trailing mode. Finally, mark a line one-third down from the front face using a pencil and rule.

2 Using the ¼in (6mm) parting tool, part in centrally at the marked line to a depth of ³⁄₁₆in (5mm). Open out slightly by taking ¹⁄₃₂in (1mm) off either side to the same depth.

3 Using a ¹⁄₁₆in (2mm) parting tool, part in just left of the right shoulder to leave ³⁄₁₆in (5mm) waste in the centre of the blank. To stop the tool from binding, open out the groove as you proceed by parting in at stages of ¼in (6mm). Withdraw the tool, move over to the left and part in, exceeding the previous cut by ¼in (6mm). Remove the tool and part in again at the first cut deeper again, continuing back and forth until you reach the correct depth.

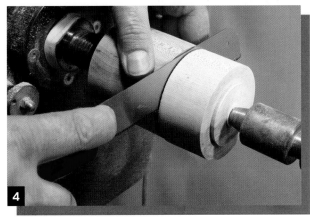

4 Stop the lathe and cut through the remaining waste with a fine-blade saw.

5 Fit the body of the box into the chuck, tighten and drill out ¼in (6mm) short of the final depth of the box using a 1in (25mm) sawtooth bit. Repeat for the lid.

6 Tape the two parts together so that the drilled sections face outwards. Weigh the item and write the date, species and weight on the tape. Store and monitor as described above. If the climate is hot and dry, then it is best to seal the end grain as a precaution.

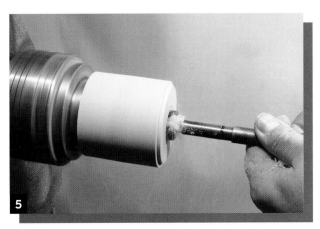

HOLLOWING THE INTERIOR

This endgrain vessel is hollowed with a spindle gouge so that the fibres of the wood are peeled from the inside out. As with any endgrain project, we work from large to small diameter for profiling the outside and from small to large diameter for hollowing the inside. The diagram below details the cutting directions for the inside and outside of the box and lid.

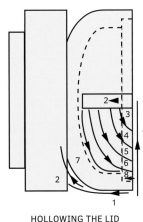

HOLLOWING THE LID

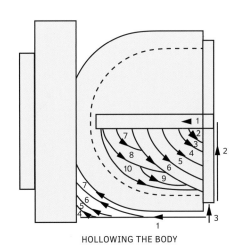

HOLLOWING THE BODY

7 Place the lid in the chuck. Mark the thickness of the lid minus ³⁄₁₆in (5mm) on a ¼in (6mm) spindle gouge, using a marker pen. Set the toolrest so the gouge tip is on centre height with the handle horizontal, flute facing up and in line with the spindle axis. Plunge the tool gently in, removing regularly to clear the shavings. Continue to full depth.

8 Take a fine cut with the gouge to clean up the front face. Mark the diameter of the base spigot minus ⅛in or so (3–4mm) onto the front face using a pencil and rule. Set the toolrest so the handle of the spindle gouge is slightly higher than the cutting tip. Rotate the flute at 45° towards you. The 10 o'clock part of the tool edge is the part that cuts as we peel outwards.

9 Enter the gouge a short distance into the drilled hole and peel outwards in an arc, using the intersection of the tool and rest as a pivot point. The location of the spigot on the box body that will fit into the lid has been marked on the face with a pencil. Hollow out as in the drawings on page 23, stopping around ¼in (6mm) from the line. If the gouge is sharp and the final cut is smooth, there will be no need to finish with a scraper.

10 Using a ½in (12mm) skew chisel horizontal on the toolrest, cut in to a depth of ³⁄₁₆in (5mm) a fraction inside the line previously parted. This is to allow for cleaning up the spigot on the roughed-out base.

11 Use callipers to check that the sides of the recess are parallel. If required, refine the sides further.

12 Finish with abrasive from 180 to 400 grit, taking care not to alter the size of the recess excessively. Apply moderate pressure to the abrasive, as excess heat will cause heat checking in the form of fine cracks, especially on dense timbers. At this stage, you can apply your chosen finish and buff the inside with kitchen towel or safety cloth.

13 Mount the base into the chuck and clean up the front face with a ¼in (6mm) spindle gouge, aiming to remove as little material as possible. Measure the recess in the lid and accurately mark this on the front face using a rule and pencil. Drill out to depth as in step 7 and hollow as in step 9. Here I am using a curved box scraper to hollow, as an alternative method. Hollow out, stopping ³⁄₁₆in (5mm) from the line. If required, sharpen the scraper and refine the inside, taking a fine scrape. Finish the inside with abrasive and sanding sealer as before.

14 Refine the spigot using a ¼in (6mm) parting tool, taking fine cuts. Check the fit with the lid until you have a fit too tight for everyday use. Finally, finish the inside of the box with abrasives from 120 to 320 grit.

15 Using 240–320 grit abrasive, finish the spigot, continually checking with the lid until you have achieved a snug fit. Finish the inside with sanding sealer and buff as before.

16 Place a piece of kitchen towel between the box and lid before jamming the lid on. Bring the tail centre up for extra security and profile the external shape using a ³⁄₈in (10mm) spindle gouge, working 'downhill' to a safe distance from the chuck and tail centre as shown on page 23.

17 Withdraw the tail centre and remove the remaining waste with the spindle gouge. Make sure you gently rub the bevel of the gouge on the face of the lid prior to starting the cut.

18 Using the toe of a skew chisel, form a small groove straddling the join. Finally, finish the box lid and body as before with abrasive and sanding sealer.

19 Fit the base over a jam chuck made from waste wood, placing kitchen towel between box and chuck to protect the internal finish. Using a ¼in (6mm) spindle gouge, refine the base profile, working down towards the base. Finally, hollow the base so the box will sit stable in use. Finish and blend with 120–400 grit, then apply your chosen finish as before.

20 Alternatively, the finish can be applied off the lathe and then buffed with a buffing system.

THREE YEW BOXES

European yew (*Taxus baccata*) is one of the most beautiful of woods. Classed as a softwood but harder than many hardwoods, it is used for furniture and decorative woodware, and is an excellent wood for turning, as Bob Chapman shows here.

WHAT YOU NEED

- Seasoned yew blanks, a little larger than the finished sizes shown (crossgrain for the Pebble box, endgrain for the others)
- Parting tool
- Bowl gouge
- Spindle gouge
- Small scraper
- Skew chisel
- 1/8in (3mm) bead-forming tool
- Rotary tool with square-end cutter
- Cyanoacrylate (superglue)
- 240–400 grit abrasive papers
- Sanding sealer
- Wire brush or abrasive discs

INTRODUCTION

Yew heartwood varies from pale orange-brown to mid-brown, sometimes stained red or purple by iron, and the sapwood is a pale creamy white, often accompanied by shades of grey at the boundary with the heartwood. Both heartwood and sapwood turn easily, sand well and take a high polish.

HISTORY

A yew growing in the churchyard at Fortingall in Perthshire, Scotland, is thought to be between 2,000 and 5,000 years old and is possibly the oldest living thing in Europe. There are several churchyard yews estimated to be around 2,000 years old, predating Christianity itself. One theory is that churches were built near yew trees to help encourage converts from the old to the new religion.

Probably the best-known use of yew was in the production of longbows, which were traditionally made from staves selected to contain both heartwood and sapwood along the length of the bow. The heartwood, which resists compression, was positioned on the inside of the bow and the sapwood, strong in tension, on the outside. These properties make a yew

bow difficult to draw but swift to spring back, sending the arrow fast and far. The skill of English bowmen was largely responsible for success in battles such as Crécy (1346) and Agincourt (1415).

For bow-making, all the natural defects that are common in yew must be avoided and only very straight-grained timber is suitable. As a result the manufacture of longbow staves is very wasteful and medieval demand for bows led to a serious decline in the number of mature yew trees. Their depletion all over Europe was partly responsible for the change from longbows to muskets as weapons of war, which occurred between about 1545 and 1595. Fortunately, churchyards seem to have been exempted from the search for 'weapons-grade' yew trees.

MAKING YEW BOXES

When sketching shapes for boxes, decide whether or not sapwood will be included. The Pebble design is so simple that the sapwood contrast is likely to increase the visual attraction of the box, whereas the other designs are more formal and a patch of sapwood would dominate the piece, leading the eye away from the primary design features of shape or texture.

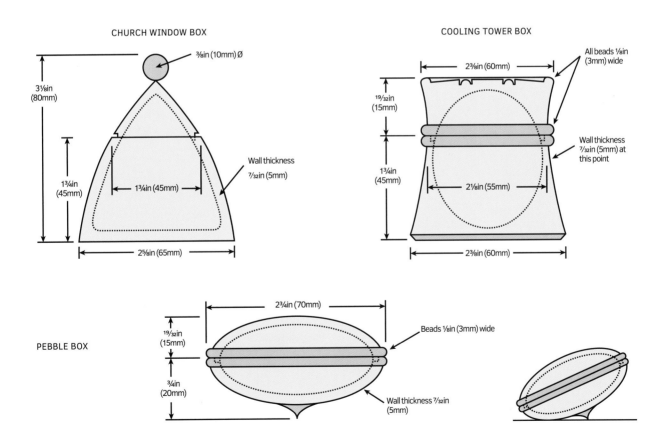

Wall thicknesses are approximate

CHURCH WINDOW BOX

1 Using the given dimensions as a guide, select a suitably sized piece of yew with spindle (endgrain) orientation. Turn this down to 2⅝in (65mm) between centres, and form dovetails on each end. Mark out a section at about 1¾in (45mm) for the box bottom and take the remainder down to a diameter a little more than 1¾in (45mm). Part off this narrower section, which will be used for the lid.

2 Use a bowl gouge to reduce the outside of the blank to the approximate shape required, maintaining the smallest diameter at just over 1¾in (45mm). The inside is rough-hollowed using a spindle gouge with its flute at about 10 o'clock, pulling it from the centre out towards the edge.

3 Yew is prone to small cracks and shakes, but you can fill these with superglue (cyanoacrylate). Use thin glue and give it time to penetrate the crack by capillary action. Allow time for the glue to set.

4 Use a small scraper to complete the shaping and refine the inside surface. This scraper has the burr honed away and is used horizontally, with the cutting edge at centre height or very slightly below. Take light cuts from the centre outwards and up the sides to the top. The curvature of the internal corners matches the shape of the scraper.

5 Sand lightly with 240 and 400-grit papers before sealing with sanding sealer. Next, use a skew chisel to cut the shallow recess to accept the box lid.

6 Mark the blank so that it can be replaced in the same position, remove it from the chuck and replace it with the lid section. Carefully turn down a short spigot to be a tight fit in the open end of the box. This requires a lot of trial and error – be patient!

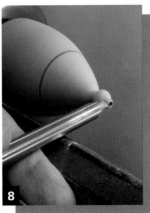

7 Fit the box onto the lid. If the fit is good, the box will stay in place when the lathe is switched on, but if in doubt, bring up the tailstock centre for extra support. With a small bowl gouge, shape the lid to match the curvature of the box. Continue until the curve flows smoothly across the joint between the pieces. Once the external shape of the lid has been established, remove the box bottom and hollow the inside of the lid, using the spindle gouge and scraper as before. Sand and seal the interior of the lid, and remove it from the chuck.

8 Replace the box body section in the chuck and refit the lid, matching the grain pattern from box to lid. No matter how good the fit, the joint between box and lid will always be visible, so make a feature of it by cutting a narrow groove on the joint line. Complete the shaping of the lid and the ball on top. If the lid slips or comes off, put a piece of tissue across the box and then reinsert the lid. This will tighten the fit enough to allow the ball to be finished.

9 With the box completed, it is now almost ready for parting off. I intend to texture the surface, but if you prefer a smooth polished surface then sand and polish before parting off.

10 It is important that the lines of the texture run vertically down the box and that they all start and end at the same level. To help with this, draw pencil lines on the box as a guide. The texturing is fairly straightforward and uses the corner of a square-end cutter in a rotary tool. This raises small splinters and wispy bits of fuzz on the wood, which can be removed with a fine wire brush or an abrasive disc with plastic bristles.

11 Texturing always looks better with well-defined start and finish lines, and to achieve this the box is returned to the lathe in order to cut in slightly at the top and bottom of the texturing with a small parting tool. To prevent the top coming off, hold it in place with some insulating tape.

12 The box is then parted off and reversed onto long-nose jaws used in expansion mode just inside the recess for the lid. This allows you to clean up the bottom of the box, taking light cuts with a small bowl gouge. After buffing, the box is finished.

PEBBLE BOX

1 For this design you'll need a piece of yew approximately 3in (75mm) diameter by 2in (50mm) thick, containing both heartwood and sapwood, with the grain running from side to side rather like a small bowl blank. Mount it between centres, then true up the blank and form a shallow ³⁄₁₆in (5mm) dovetail spigot on each side. Then, using a narrow parting tool, divide the blank into two slightly unequal parts, approximately ⁵⁄₈ and ¾in (16 and 19mm) thick.

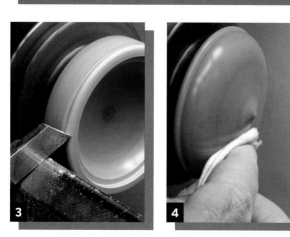

2 The deeper part becomes the box body. Holding it by the spigot, hollow it out with a gouge, refine with a scraper, then sand and seal and cut a recess to receive the lid. Take care to allow enough wall thickness for the beads, which mark the joint between lid and box.

3 Use a ⅛in (3mm) bead-forming tool to make a bead right on the very edge of the box, blending the curve of the bead into the flat area where the top and bottom will meet.

4 Reverse the work and hold it by expanding the chuck jaws into the recess that was formed for the lid. Using a small gouge, complete the underside, forming a small point which will tip the box sideways. This finishes the box bottom, which is now sanded and sealed ready for buffing later.

5 The box lid is made in a similar way, taking care when cutting the spigot to fit the box bottom. The lid is hollowed as before and can be reversed in the jaws and gripped gently by the spigot, using tape to protect it if necessary, while the upper surface is completed. The two parts are then combined into the finished box.

COOLING TOWER BOX

1 Starting with a suitably sized endgrain blank, form a cylinder of 2⅝in (65mm) diameter and about 3in (75mm) long with a dovetail spigot on each end. Mark the division between body and lid and part the lid section off, leaving the body in the chuck. Form the bead around the top edge, hollow the box body and cut a recess to accept the lid. None of the dimensions are critical, but refer to the measured drawing for guidance. Note the shape of the interior of the box: a smooth curve is easier to shape than sharp corners and has the added advantage that it makes small items easier to get out of the box.

2 Repeat this process for the lid, forming a spigot that is a tight fit in the box body. Replace the body in the chuck and insert the lid. If the fit is tight the lid can be worked on without coming loose; if it won't stay put, hold it directly in the chuck, gripping the spigot in the jaws and using tape to protect the spigot if necessary. Turn the top of the lid smooth and level and form the bead on the outer edge.

3 With a small gouge, shape the lid top and edge down to the bottom of the beads, adding extra beads if desired. In the same way, shape the side of the box down to meet the bottom of the lower bead.

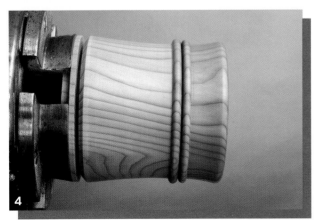

4 Examine the profile and ensure that the curve of the sides is continuous from the body, through the beads into the lid. Part off the box body and reverse it, holding it with the chuck jaws expanded into the lid recess. Clean up the bottom of the box with a small gouge, then sand, seal and polish and the job's done.

KITCHEN STORAGE JARS

These simple, hygienic containers by Nick Arnull can be made in a range of sizes to suit the items you like to keep in your store cupboard. They are a huge improvement on flimsy supermarket packaging, and their airtight lids work much better than those annoying resealable tapes that always seem to lose their stick.

WHAT YOU NEED
• Beech blanks a little larger than the sizes in the cutting list
• Acrylic tubes as per cutting list
• Bandsaw
• Non-toxic rubber nitrile O-rings, ³⁄₁₆in (5mm) thick (one per jar)
• ³⁄₈in (10mm) round skew chisel
• ³⁄₈in (10mm) spindle gouge
• ³⁄₈in (10mm) long-grind bowl gouge
• ¹⁄₁₆in (1.5mm) parting tool
• ¹⁄₈in (3mm) parting tool
• ³⁄₄in (20mm) square-end box scraper
• 1¹⁄₄in (32mm) spindle roughing gouge
• Double-sided carpet tape
• Soft pencil
• Silicone adhesive
• Food-safe oil
• Small round-nose scraper

INTRODUCTION

I have used acrylic tubes for the insides of the containers to provide a food-safe environment for dried foods to be stored in. I used English beech (*Fagus sylvatica*) for the wooden components, including the lids. The seals are made using simple non-toxic rubber O-rings which are readily available; these are set into a small groove in the lid or bung.

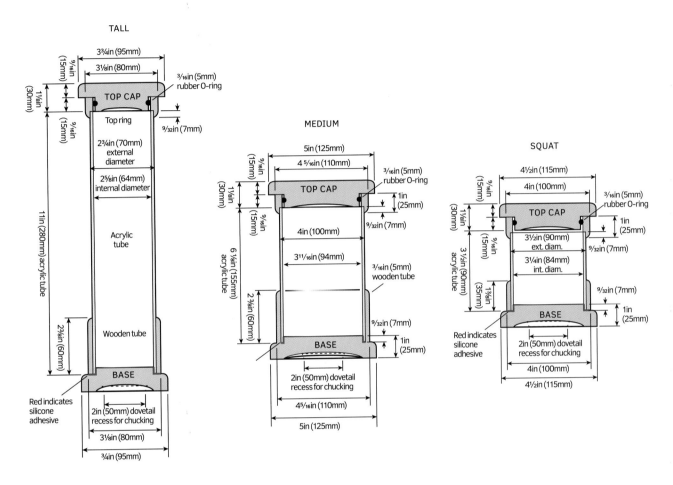

	MEDIUM	SQUAT	TALL
Base (side grain)	5⅛ × 5⅛ × 1in (130 x 130 x 25mm)	4¾ × 4¾ × 1in (120 × 120 × 25mm)	4 × 4 × 1in (100 × 100 × 25mm)
Wooden tube (end grain)	4½ × 4½ × 2¾in (115 × 115× 70mm)	4⅛ × 4⅛× 1¾in (105 × 105 × 45mm)	3¼ × 3¼ × 2¾in (85 × 85 × 70mm)
Top ring (end grain)	4½ × 4½ × 1¾in (115 × 115 × 45mm)	4⅛ × 4⅛ × 1¾in (105 × 105 × 45mm)	3¼ × 3 ¼ × 1¾in (85 × 85 × 45mm)
Lid (side grain)	5⅛ × 5⅛ × 1⅜in (130 × 130 × 35mm)	4¾ × 4¾ × 1⅜in (120 × 120 × 35mm)	4 × 4 × 1⅜in (100 × 100 × 35mm)
Acrylic tube	6⅛in (155mm) × 4in (100mm) diameter	3½in (90mm) × 3½in (90mm) diameter	11in (280mm) × 2⅜in (70mm) diameter

The instructions given are for the medium container, made from 4in (100mm) diameter acrylic tube. The process is the same for the different sizes; see the drawings for measurements.

1 Begin by cutting the acrylic storage tubes to length as per the drawings. Use a fine-toothed blade on your bandsaw (6tpi or finer) and reduce the speed to the slowest setting. Wrap the tube with masking tape to reduce the risk of chipping at the edge.

2 Centre and mount your blank to a faceplate with double-sided carpet tape, using the tailstock to centre the blank. True the base and create a 2in (50mm) dovetail recess to fit onto your chuck.

3 Reverse-chuck the blank and true the edge and face using a ⅜in (10mm) spindle gouge.

4 Create a 9⁄32in (7mm) long spigot using a ¼in (6mm) parting tool to fit snugly inside the acrylic tube.

5 Radius the corner to soften the edge of the base using a ⅜in (10mm) spindle gouge, then shear-scrape the surface with a ⅜in (10mm) round skew chisel.

6 Sand through all the grades of abrasive to a good finish. Apply a food-safe oil, then burnish the surface to remove the excess oil.

7 Reverse-chuck the base and hold the spigot in large jaws while you remove the dovetail recess. Dish the base with a ⅜in (10mm) spindle gouge. Sand and finish the base.

8 Mount your blank between centres and make it round using a 1¼in (32mm) spindle roughing gouge, then create a 2in (50mm) spigot to fit into your chuck.

9 Accurately mark the internal diameter of the acrylic tube on the surface of the blank – I did this with a pair of dividers.

10 Plunge into the wood inside the previously marked line using a ⅛in (3mm) parting tool; this will set the diameter of the opening.

11 Using a spindle gouge, drill a hole into the end grain. Alternatively, this can be completed using a drill bit mounted into a Jacobs chuck held in the tailstock.

12 True the outside to a diameter of 4½in (115mm); this needs to be parallel.

13 Soften the top edge using a ⅜in (10mm) spindle gouge and refine the surface with a ⅜in (10mm) round skew chisel.

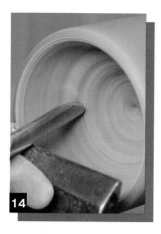

14 Next, you need to remove the waste timber from the centre of the blank using a ⅜in (10mm) long-grind bowl gouge, working from the centre out; this will allow the timber to be removed easily.

15 Refine the inside wall with a ¾in (20mm) square-end box scraper to allow the acrylic tube to fit snugly inside the wooden tube. At this stage, take care to produce a good cut from the tool as the wall is beginning to become thin.

16 You can now sand, seal and finish the wooden tube.

17 Using a soft pencil, mark 2⅜in (60mm) from the top along the side of the tube, then part through at this point using a ¹⁄₁₆in (1.5mm) parting tool. Lightly hold the piece as the tube parts from the waste wood.

18 To turn the top ring, repeat the process as for the bottom ring, but this time add a shoulder using the square-end box scraper. Turn a recess the same diameter as the tube and ⁹⁄₃₂in (7mm) deep; this ledge will stop the tube sliding through the wooden ring. Sand and finish as before, then measure 1in (25mm) along the side and part from the waste timber.

19 Remount the ring onto the chuck, using the recess previously turned as the chucking method. Do not overtighten the chuck jaws, as this will crack the wooden ring. Now soften the inside top, as this will become the opening of the container.

20 To turn the top cap, mount your blank onto a wooden faceplate using double-sided carpet tape, then turn a spigot ⁹⁄₁₆in (15mm) long; this will need to fit loosely inside the wooden top ring. Next, using a small round-nose scraper, create a groove which will later be fitted with a non-toxic O-ring to create the seal for the container. Fit the O-ring and check the fit inside the top ring, as you need to get it just right – it needs to fit but not be too tight.

21 You now need to dish the centre using a ³⁄₈in (10mm) long-grind bowl gouge, then sand and finish.

22 You can now remove the blank from the lathe and remount in the chuck using the spigot that was previously turned. Next, you need to soften the top edge of the piece to match the detail on the base of the jar. You can now sand and finish.

23 Assemble the jar using silicone adhesive to join the components together, then allow to dry.

HANDY HINTS

- Use only food-safe products and finishes for this project.

- Keep the design simple to avoid food traps.

- Ensure that the lids are ergonomic and easy to remove.

- Ensure there is a smooth transition where the timber joins the acrylic tube.

- Sand and finish the inside of the timber tubes before removing them from the lathe.

- Small marks on the acrylic tubes can be polished out using an automotive scratch remover or a microabrasive medium.

BOX COLLECTION

Here are ten endgrain shapes by Mark Baker for you to grapple with, presenting a logical progression in complexity.

INTRODUCTION

This selection of boxes assumes knowledge of the basic techniques covered in the book so far. If you can make these boxes then there is no shape outside your reach or scope. One project uses a separate contrasting piece of wood for a finial; you can add finials to the other designs if you choose.

BOX 1

This cylindrical box in lignum vitae (*Guaiacum officinale*) can be made higher, shallower, wider as you wish. The lid detailing provides much scope for you to personalize the box. Note the radiused corner details. The bead on the join line helps disguise any movement.

The tiny beads are created by taking a ⅛in (3mm) parting tool and cutting a groove in the end of it, using the corner of a bench grinder which has been very slightly radiused. This is then cleaned up to a full U-form with a rotary burr. The bead produced will be between ⁵⁄₆₄ and ³⁄₃₂in (2 and 2.5mm) diameter. The modified tool is no longer suitable for use as a parting tool, but as a micro-bead-forming tool it is excellent.

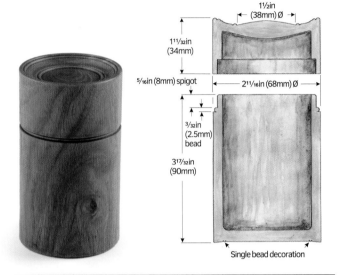

Single bead decoration

WHAT YOU NEED

- ¾in (19mm) spindle roughing gouge
- ⅜in (10mm) spindle gouge
- ⅜in (10mm) beading/parting tool
- 1in (25mm) angled side-cut scraper
- ⅜in (10mm) French-curve scraper
- Micro-bead-forming tool (see text)
- Abrasive to 400 grit
- Spray lacquer
- Paste wax

BOX 2

This box in mulberry (*Morus* sp.) has, I think, more visual presence than the previous box. Like many successful designs, it is a simple modification of an earlier box. The lid is easily gripped in the hand and there is a gentle friction fit between lid and base. The join is delineated by a small parting-tool cut to minimize any visual implications of wood movement; I do not think it affects the visual flow of the curve.

The beading on the top was cut with the spindle gouge ground to a fingernail profile. If you are having trouble creating uniform beads, try adjusting them with a beading-and-parting tool used as a scraper. The finish is not so clean, but is easy to sand to a good finish. Be gentle with the sanding – if you are too aggressive you can flatten off the detail.

WHAT YOU NEED

- ¾in (19mm) spindle roughing gouge
- ⅜in (10mm) spindle gouge
- ⅜in (10mm) beading/parting tool
- 1in (25mm) angled side-cut scraper
- ⅜in (10mm) French-curve scraper
- Micro-bead-forming tool (see text)
- Abrasive to 400 grit
- Spray lacquer
- Paste wax

BOX 3

This box in rippled maple (*Acer saccharum*) is a hybrid of the two previous designs. The join is this time accentuated with a gentle undercut curve; the grain misalignment – which is minor anyway – is partially obscured by the join. The curved internal form allows you to slide out small items such as rings. The inside shape does not mimic the external form. The contrast is a nice surprise when people open the box – try to challenge those preconceptions! Again, the lid is a gentle suction fit.

Careful sanding is required on the gently domed top so that it forms one continuous curve with no ridging. Try using a medium-density rubber pad as an interface for the abrasive. The more of the abrasive surface that is in contact with the work, the purer the form. I left the dome clear of too much detail, so the ripple figuring could be shown to its fullest extent.

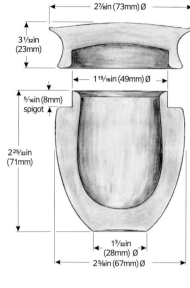

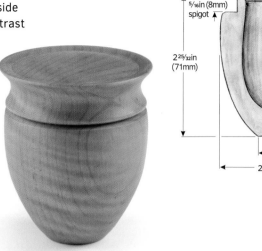

WHAT YOU NEED

- ¾in (19mm) spindle roughing gouge
- ⅜in (10mm) spindle gouge
- ⅜in (10mm) beading/parting tool
- 1in (25mm) French-curve scraper
- Abrasive to 600 grit
- Lacquer, buffed with a polishing wheel

BOX 4

This needle case shows that boxes do not have to be large to be useful. The joint fit is tighter than the ones described earlier, but not so much so that you have to be Superman to open it. It just needs to be a firm fit so the lid does not come off accidentally. You could also consider thread-chasing to create a different type of joint. The wood is an Australian burr, but as to what species, I have drawn a blank – no pun intended – as it came in a mixed pack of offcuts.

The inside bore is not turned but drilled with a twist drill. This will create a clean finish at the bottom of this dense timber and, depending on the make, should also create a clean bore as it cuts, thus minimizing the need for sanding. Using a scraper on the inside should not be necessary.

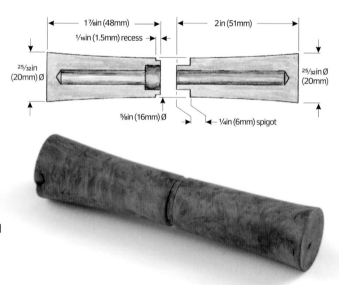

WHAT YOU NEED

- ¾in (19mm) spindle roughing gouge
- ⅜in (10mm) spindle gouge
- ⅜in (10mm) beading/parting tool
- Pillar drill or Jacobs chuck with ¼in (6mm) drill bit
- Abrasive to 600 grit
- Oil finish

BOX 5

This Chinese-style ginger jar is one of my all-time favourite shapes. It can be used for cookies if made large, or kept small for more personal items like rings and necklaces. The wood is European cherry (*Prunus avium*), and the pronounced colour and striped grain pattern add a bit of drama. The lid is a soft or slide-over fit, which enables it to be lifted off without holding on to the base.

You will need an articulated or swan-neck hollowing tool to create the undercut shoulder. Remember to keep the straight section of the tool shank in contact with the toolrest. If you do not, the control point of the tool is shifted and it is difficult to control. Make multiple light cuts when hollowing out, and make sweeping refining cuts to clean up the surface prior to sanding. Sanding is done by hand, using abrasive wrapped around a stick.

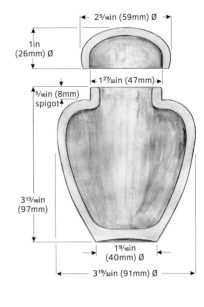

WHAT YOU NEED

- ¾in (19mm) spindle roughing gouge
- ⅜in (10mm) spindle gouge
- ⅜in (10mm) beading/parting tool
- 1in (25mm) French-curve scraper
- Articulated or swan-neck hollowing tool
- Abrasive to 600 grit
- Lacquer, buffed with a polishing wheel

BOX 6

This design is a pedestal box for a ring. The lid simply sits in a groove and lifts off with the minimum of fuss. It is made from boxwood (*Buxus sempervirens*) and incorporates the natural edge of the log. If you don't have boxwood, look at other woods that have a small bark and pith area. Yew (*Taxus* spp.), fruitwood branches (*Prunus, Malus* spp.) and so on are great for this type of project, as are some burrs, especially the small Australian ones.

The hardest part of natural-edge work is cutting through the hit-or-miss section of the irregular branch shape, where the tool is not always in contact with the wood. The trick is to glide the tool through the cut, maintaining pressure on the rest and keeping gentle bevel contact with the wood. Too much pressure will give a juddering cut, which may result in splitting.

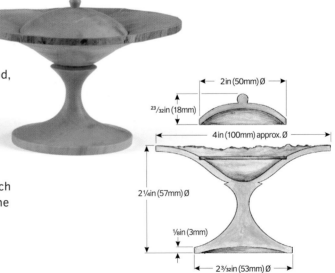

WHAT YOU NEED

- ¾in (19mm) spindle roughing gouge
- ⅜in (10mm) spindle gouge
- ⅜in (10mm) beading/parting tool
- 1in (25mm) French-curve scraper
- Abrasive to 600 grit
- Oil finish

BOX 7

This box is made from burr elm (*Ulmus procera*) and African blackwood (*Dalbergia melanoxylon*). The heart shape is the hardest form included in this chapter, because of changing grain direction and difficulty of access. Most of the hollowing can be done with a gouge, using the hollowing tool of your choice to finish off under the shoulder. The lid is a loose-fitting sit-in type, as people are bound to pick it up by the finial. This means that the finial must not be too delicate.

When turning the finial between centres, create a round tenon to fit in the Jacobs chuck, so the finial can be shaped with the tailstock as support. Cut from the tailstock back towards the chuck. The last cut should be made after releasing the tailstock, allowing you to clean up the tip of the finial. I did this by supporting the finial in my left hand and making two delicate cuts to remove the section which was left by the tailstock.

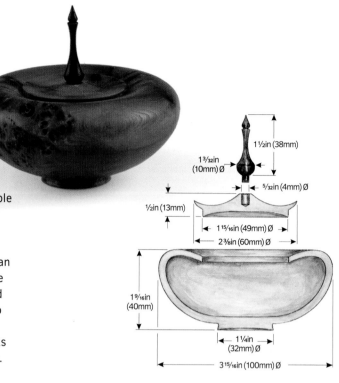

WHAT YOU NEED

- ¾in (19mm) spindle roughing gouge
- ⅜in (10mm) spindle gouge
- ⅜in (10mm) beading/parting tool
- 1in (25mm) French-curve scraper
- Articulated or swan-neck hollowing tool
- Jacobs chuck and 5/32in (4mm) drill bit
- Abrasive to 600 grit
- Oil finish

BOX 8

This box is made from one of the American red oaks (*Quercus* sp.). The base should cause no problems, but the tricky part is working with the square edges for the top of the lid. I have turned them so the wings point upwards, but you could have them coming out square to the sides, or pointing downwards. The cutting action required for this is similar to that of the natural-edge piece above. You must cut in such a way as to protect the wing tips at all times.

To finish off the top I use tissue paper placed over the spigot, onto which the lid sits to ensure a snug fit while turning – in effect, a jam chuck. Sand the lid while stationary to make sure you don't catch your fingers on the spinning corners. I have done this and it hurts!

WHAT YOU NEED

- ¾in (19mm) spindle roughing gouge
- ⅜in (10mm) spindle gouge
- ⅜in (10mm) beading/parting tool
- 1in (25mm) French-curve scraper
- Abrasive to 400 grit
- Oil finish

BOX 9

This tactile design is one that I keep coming back to. It is a variant of a rugby ball. This one is made from London plane (*Platanus hybrida*), whose clearly defined rays add a new visual dimension. You can see why quartersawn plane is referred to as lacewood. Having no base to sit on, this type of box rolls in an arc and settles once the heaviest part is at the bottom. In a previous version I placed micro beads all the way around it and just left the ends clean.

Because there is a mating spigot and recess, the internal form is best left a little thicker than normal, until after the recess and joining spigot have been created.

I tried applying a high-gloss lacquer to this box, but the gloss, I thought, diminished the appearance of the ray figuring, so instead I opted for oil.

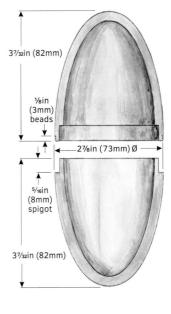

3⁷/₃₂in (82mm)

¹/₈in (3mm) beads

2⁷/₈in (73mm) Ø

5¹⁵/₁₆in (8mm) spigot

3⁷/₃₂in (82mm)

WHAT YOU NEED

- ¾in (19mm) spindle roughing gouge
- ³/₈in (10mm) spindle gouge
- ³/₈in (10mm) beading/parting tool
- 1in (25mm) French-curve scraper
- Micro-bead-forming tool
- Abrasive to 600 grit
- Oil finish

BOX 10

Spheres are a popular shape for boxes. This one is made from yew (*Taxus baccata*) branch wood and has a loose ring to sit on so it doesn't roll away. The biggest problem is how to make the joining spigot. Again, the wall thickness should be left thick until the spigot and corresponding recess have been cut, then the wall can be reduced to the thickness you desire.

The loose ring is made in a contrasting timber using a bead-forming tool, or a dedicated captive-ring-cutting tool. It adds a nice contrast and also allows the sphere to perform a practical function.

Yew heat-checks quickly, so sand through the grades with a light touch.

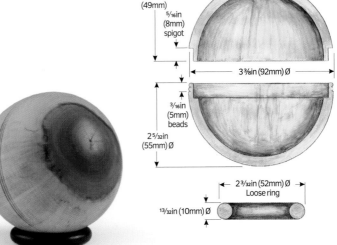

1¹⁵/₁₆in (49mm)

⁵/₁₆in (8mm) spigot

3³/₈in (92mm) Ø

³/₁₆in (5mm) beads

2⁵/₃₂in (55mm) Ø

2³/₃₂in (52mm) Ø Loose ring

1³/₃₂in (10mm) Ø

WHAT YOU NEED

- ¾in (19mm) spindle roughing gouge
- ³/₈in (10mm) spindle gouge
- ³/₈in (10mm) beading/parting tool
- 1in (25mm) French-curve scraper
- Micro bead-forming tool
- ³/₈in (10mm) bead-forming tool or captive-ring tool
- Abrasive to 600 grit
- Spray lacquer finish

OFFSET LIDDED FORM

The wood used here by Mark Sanger is spalted beech (*Fagus sylvatica*), with the simple addition of V-grooves as a surface texture. The lid insert and finial are produced from a contrasting wood, anjan (*Hardwickia binata*); this adds interest by making a statement of the handle but also complements the darker tones of the spalted beech.

WHAT YOU NEED

- Seasoned blank in parallel-grained spalted beech (*Fagus sylvatica*), 4in (100mm) square × 8in (200mm) long
- A similar blank, 1in (25mm) square × 3¼in (80mm) long
- Seasoned blank in parallel-grained anjan (*Hardwickia binata*), 1in (25mm) square × 2⅜in (60mm) long
- A similar blank, 4in (100mm) square × ⁵⁄₁₆in (8mm) thick
- 1in (25mm) spindle roughing gouge
- ⅜in (10mm) bowl gouge
- ⅜in (10mm) spindle gouge with fingernail profile
- ½in (12mm) skew chisel
- ¼in (6mm) parting tool
- ⅛in (3mm) parting tool
- 1½in (40mm) sawtooth bit
- Endgrain hollowing tool
- Round hollowing tool
- Finishing scraper attachment or 1in (25mm) round-nose scraper
- ¼in (6mm) point tool
- Fine-blade saw
- Power carver or chisel
- Pillar drill and ⅜in (10mm) spur bit
- Soft-jaw vice
- Callipers
- Vernier callipers
- Abrasives, 120-400 grit
- Finishing oil
- Medium-viscosity cyanoacrylate glue (superglue)
- PPE: face mask, respirator/dust mask, extraction

INTRODUCTION

Looking at ways to alter the composition of my lidded forms, in which the finial is central to the axis of the main form, I came up with the first in this series – my signature chilli form. Like any woodturning project, it can be used as a starting point for further exploration.

The markings in the wood needed only a plain finish to impart a soft sheen, complementing the natural beauty of the wood; however, you can use the finish of your choice. In this project I used an endgrain hollowing tool, but for smaller forms, a ⅜in (10mm) spindle gouge can be used instead. So if you don't have a hollowing tool, just reduce the height of the piece to suit what you do have.

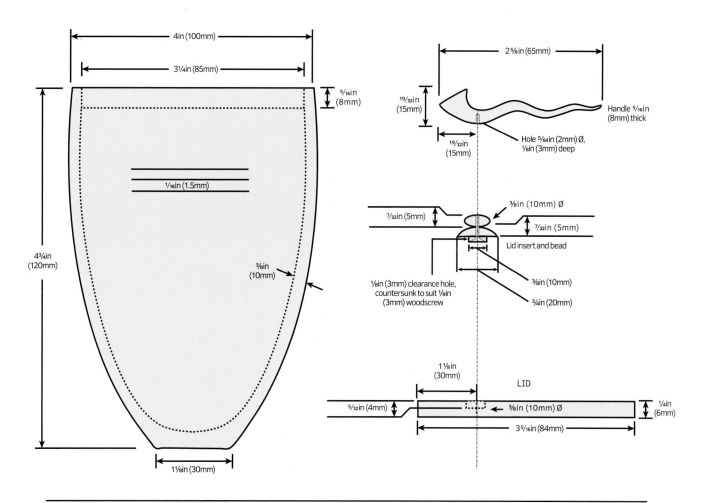

1 Mount your blank between centres and rough down to the round using a 1in (25mm) spindle roughing gouge. You can then clean up both ends to a safe distance from the drive and tail centres using a ¼in (6mm) parting tool.

2 Produce a spigot at the tail-centre end of the blank using the ¼in (6mm) parting tool and refine using the toe of a ½in (12mm) skew chisel in scraper mode, to suit the profile of your chuck jaws.

3 Reverse the blank and tighten in the chuck, then clean up the front face using a ½in (12mm) skew chisel to refine the finish of the piece. Using a ¼in (6mm) parting tool, produce a shoulder which is approximately 5⁄16in (8mm) deep by ½in (12mm) wide.

4 Finish the front face of the blank and the parted shoulder with abrasive from 120 to 320 grit.

5 Using a ⅜in (10mm) bowl gouge, rough down the outside profile of the form. At this stage, do not turn the lower section towards the base to less than half the diameter of the blank, as you need to retain strength for the hollowing.

6 Refine the finish with a 1in (25mm) skew chisel, but do not work further than two-thirds down from the rim as the lower section will be profiled further at a later stage.

7 Using a ⅛in (3mm) parting tool, part the front face from the shoulder, leaving about 1⁄64in (0.5mm) remaining as a reference for the size of the recess into which this will be reinserted once hollowed.

8 Drill out to depth using a 1½in (40mm) sawtooth bit. Mark the depth on the drill shaft with a permanent marker as a guide.

9 Now measure the thickness of the previously parted lid piece. Using a ¼in (6mm) spindle gouge, open out the entrance of the form, producing a recess for this to sit down into. At this stage, turn to a depth ⅛in (3mm) shallower than the thickness of the insert and stop short of the registration material previously left.

10 Next, using the toe of a ½in (12mm) skew chisel in scraping mode, plunge-cut with the tip trailing to gradually open out the recess. Regularly check the fit with the actual lid until it fits to the full depth of the recess and just a few millimetres are protruding above the rim. Remove the lid and set to one side.

11 Using an endgrain hollowing tool, hollow out the box body, leaving a shoulder approximately ³⁄₁₆in (5mm) wide for the lid to sit on.

12 Refine the surface with a round-nose scraper and finish this, together with the recess, with abrasive to 320 grit. Be careful not to remove too much material from the recess into which the lid will sit, or the fit will become loose. I generally finish the recess with 240 and 320 grit, forgoing the 120 and 180 grits as they can be too aggressive in a small area.

13 Stick a strip of masking tape across the top of the lid, leaving 2in (50mm) extra each side. Turn the lid upside down and insert into the recess so that the underside of the lid faces outwards with the masking tape running out each side. Twist each end of the tape and stick to the outside of the box body. The tape is not to secure the lid in place but to give a means of removing it once finished. If the fit has become loose due to sanding, then sandwich kitchen towel or similar between the lid and shoulder to fill the gap and secure the lid again with the tape. The lid should now be protruding from the rim a few millimetres, as the internal shoulder has yet to be turned to full depth. Use the ³⁄₈in (10mm) spindle gouge to clean up what will be the underside of the lid; by making sure the bevel is gently rubbing, positive force is applied to the lid, helping to keep it in place.

14 Use a point tool to add detail to the underside of the lid, but don't cut in too deep. Finish the face and detail with abrasive from 120 to 320 grit. Finally, remove the lid from the form by peeling off the masking tape and gently pulling out.

15 Using a ½in (12mm) skew chisel horizontal with the cutting edge trailing, plunge-cut the toe into the face of the internal shoulder, taking it to full depth – this being the thickness of the lid plus ⁵⁄₆₄in (2mm) – which allows the lid to sit slightly below the rim of the box. Again, check for fit with masking tape attached to the edge of the lid or it may get stuck down inside. Finish the inside with 120–320 grit abrasive. If you find it difficult to finish down inside, wrap or stick the abrasive to a length of ½in (12mm) dowel, which allows you to reach deeper into the form.

16 Using a ⅜in (10mm) bowl gouge, blend the lower section into the base.

17 Refine the outside with a ½in (12mm) skew chisel, working downhill at all times.

18 Use a ¼in (6mm) point tool to produce equally spaced grooves two-thirds of the way down the outside. The remainder will be added once the base profile has been blended.

19 Finish the grooves with abrasive from 180 to 320 grit, folding in half and using the edge to get into the base.

20 Produce a friction or jam chuck from waste wood to fit inside the top of the form. Reverse the form onto this and bring up the tail centre for support. Using a ¼in (6mm) spindle gouge, refine the lower section and shape the base, undercutting so that the form will sit without rocking once parted from the waste. Leave around ⅜in (10mm) diameter of waste at this stage.

21 Continue the grooves to the base of the form using the ¼in (6mm) point tool.

22 Reduce the speed of the lathe to around 500rpm. Use the ¼in (6mm) spindle gouge to reduce the remaining waste to around ³⁄₁₆in (5mm), working downhill from the waste into the base. Stop the lathe and cut through the remaining wood with a fine-blade saw.

23 Use a power carver or sharp chisel to refine the base. Use a small sanding arbor with 180 grit abrasive, glued into a waste piece of wood in the chuck of the lathe. Finally, finish the box by hand to 320 grit, rubbing in line with the grain.

24 Mark on the face of the lid the location for the recess into which the handle will be glued. Using a ⅜in (10mm) spur bit in a pillar drill, drill to a depth of ⁵⁄₃₂in (4mm). I use a short-spur bit, as a standard bit will often protrude through the lid. If using an ordinary bit, grind down the spur to reduce the height, and reduce the speed of the pillar drill. Drilling to such a small depth removes the problem of the drill wandering, so the spur is not so critical here.

25 Now rough out a contrasting blank to the round and mount in the chuck. Using a ¼in (6mm) parting tool, clean up the front face, and with the aid of callipers set with a Vernier or rule, produce two shoulders, the first being from the front face ⅜in (10mm) diameter by ⅛in (3mm) wide, which will fit into the drilled recess in the lid, and the second measuring ¾in (20mm) diameter by ¾in (20mm) wide.

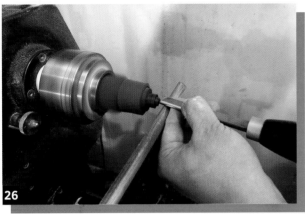

26 Using the toe of a ½in (12mm) skew chisel, countersink to suit a standard ⅛in (3mm) cross-head wood screw. Line up the point of the toe with the centre of the blank and gently push in. Alternatively, an engineer's pilot drill in a Jacobs chuck can be used.

27 Using a ⅛in (3mm) twist drill, drill through the lid to produce a clearance hole for the screw. Here I am using a bit glued into a small home-made wooden handle, but one in a Jacobs chuck held in the tail centre can be used if preferred.

28 Using a ½in (12mm) skew chisel, radius the top profile of the form, reducing the material to around ¾₆in (5mm). Remember there is a hole drilled through the centre, so don't cut in too far. You can now finish with 320-grit abrasive.

29 Continue with the toe of the skew chisel and reduce the remaining material with the lathe set at around 500rpm, then part off.

30 Produce a bead ⅜in (10mm) diameter by ³/₁₆in (5mm) thick by roughing down and mounting the small beech blank in the chuck. Produce a spigot at the front ⅜in (10mm) diameter by 1in (25mm) wide using a ¼in (6mm) parting tool. Drill a hole through the centre using the ⅛in (3mm) twist drill. Mark the thickness of the bead and the centre on the outside of the dimensioned blank with a pencil and, with either a ½in (12mm) skew chisel or a ¼in (6mm) spindle gouge, turn the profile of the bead to the right of the centreline and finish with 320-grit abrasive. Continue to the left of the centreline with the skew chisel, producing the bead to the same profile. Stop regularly to check the profile. Finish with 320-grit abrasive, part the bead from the waste and blend this area by hand with abrasive to 320 grit.

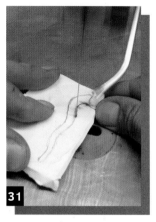

31 Draw your finial shape onto a ⁵/₁₆in (8mm) thick piece of contrasting wood, the same as for the lid insert. The grain of the wood should run through the length of the handle. Cut out using a scrollsaw or fretsaw.

32 Refine the finial with 180-grit abrasive affixed to a sanding arbor in a waste piece of wood held in the chuck. Set the lathe speed to 2,500rpm and refine the contours by hand from 180 to 320 grit. To do this, simply fold the abrasive into a tight tube, or use abrasive stuck around small sections of dowel, the radius of which is used to produce the smooth curves.

33 Mark the location for the screw hole on the underside of the handle with a pencil, then a bradawl, to give a start point for the drill. Clamp the handle in a soft-jaw vice, positioned for the hole to be drilled perpendicular to the handle. Using a ⁵/₆₄in (2mm) wood bit in a pillar drill, drill out to depth as shown, with masking tape wrapped around the bit itself as a depth gauge.

34 Apply several coats of finishing oil to the main form, lid and remaining parts, but do not let any enter the hole in the handle.

35 Place a ⅛in (3mm) wood screw through the insert and bead. Cut it to length using strong wire cutters so that about ⅛in (3mm) is protruding beyond the bead. Assemble the parts using a cross-head screwdriver. If the screw needs to be shortened further, use the cutters. Finally, drip medium-viscosity superglue into the hole in the handle and tighten all parts. Make sure the handle is perpendicular to the grain direction of the lid.

RECYCLED YARRAN FORM

Don't be afraid to review your old work. In this unusual project by Andrew Potocnik, an unsatisfactory piece is ingeniously reworked and given a new lease of life. Some interesting technical challenges are solved in the process.

WHAT YOU NEED

- Existing hollow form suitable for reworking
- Spear-point scraper
- Skew chisel
- ¼in (6mm) gouge
- Spindle gouge with fingernail grind
- Parting tool
- Chatter tool
- Broad, curved scraper
- Improvised hollowing tools
- Diamond-point scraper
- Drill and bits
- Pliers
- Variety of abrasives
- Glue gun
- Cyanoacrylate (superglue)

INTRODUCTION

Sometimes you look back on an old piece of work and think, yes, that bit of wood deserved better. But how do you find a way of remounting a finished piece on the lathe, especially when one of the key aims of modern woodturning is to disguise how the object was held on the lathe in the first place?

A small hollow form I'd turned some time ago teased me into giving it a new life. The figure in the wood was vivid, the colour deep, but the form was wanting. To convert this piece into something better required a fair bit of lateral thinking about how to improve it, but most importantly, how to hold the little critter on the lathe while I did my best to improve it.

There isn't anything wrong with re-evaluating old work to see what you once thought was OK but no longer agree with; and likewise, don't be scared to challenge your own perceptions of aesthetics.

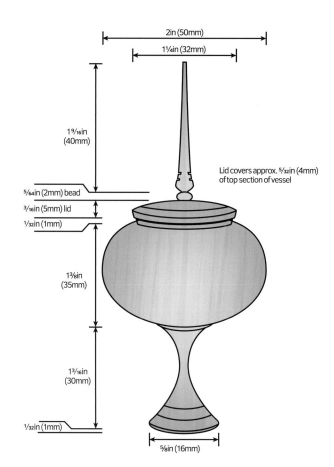

2in (50mm)
1¼in (32mm)

1⁹⁄₁₆in (40mm)

Lid covers approx. ⁵⁄₃₂in (4mm) of top section of vessel

⁵⁄₆₄in (2mm) bead
³⁄₁₆in (5mm) lid
¹⁄₃₂in (1mm)

1³⁄₈in (35mm)

1³⁄₁₆in (30mm)

¹⁄₃₂in (1mm)

⁵⁄₈in (16mm)

1 Measuring about 1¾in (45mm) in diameter, the form made of yarran (*Acacia homalophylla*, found in outback New South Wales and Queensland) had distorted minimally since turning about six months earlier. I felt it had hidden potential and I wanted to explore recycling the piece.

2 To begin reshaping it I decided to grip the piece by its flat base, so I cut a tapered recess into a scrap piece of wood mounted in a scroll chuck. The bottom of the recess would align the form so it could spin truly, while the tapered sides were needed to centre the tapered form in the carrier. The only way to get this right is to push the form into the carrier, rotate the spindle of your lathe and see whether the form runs as close to centre as possible. This takes several attempts before you'll get it right.

3 While this is happening, plug in your heat-sensitive glue gun until the glue is really hot and runny, because that's what will hold the form in its carrier and allow it to spin truly. I used a heat gun to warm both the carrier and the piece, so the glue remained pliable long enough for the form to be centred. If the glue cools too quickly you may find your work is incorrectly positioned, and you need to remove all the glue before attempting the process again. Once mounted, the slightly distorted profile was trimmed with a shear scraper until a more pleasing outline was achieved, then sanded to blend in with the existing form.

4 Next, I felt the form needed a band of texturing to create a visual break. I cut two V-grooves with a diamond-point scraper to define the borders of this band.

5 A chatter tool was then used to apply texture to the band.

6 With the top portion completed, I needed to reverse the form ready for work on its base. Using a scrap piece of material held in my chuck, I turned a spigot similar to the opening in the form, and cut a curved surface into the carrier, similar to the top of the form. The opening of the form had distorted since initial turning and had not been reshaped this time round. Heat-sensitive glue would secure the form to the carrier, so the two did not have to match perfectly. A couple of dabs of really hot glue to preheated surfaces, and the form was attached ready for further work. Keep in mind, this piece was only 1¾in (45mm) in diameter. Larger pieces would have to be firmly attached to their carriers – and never forget to use your tailstock as an auxiliary method of holding work in place. The photo shows how the form looked once the base had been reshaped and sanded.

7 To give the new form greater presence, I felt it needed a stand that would raise it up high and show off all the wonderful grain. I chose a piece of highly figured ringed gidgee (*Acacia cambagei*), which I held in another scroll chuck and turned down to an elegant shape. Sanded and parted free – with an undercut on the upper surface – it was ready to attach to the yarran form that was still in place on its carrier, held in another chuck, which was now returned to the lathe.

8 With the live centre removed from the tailstock, I used a flat piece of wood to push the quill forward and thereby clamp the stem in place while some carefully applied CA adhesive (superglue) bonded the two pieces together. The new form was now starting to take shape.

9 Now to make the lid. With timber gripped in a scroll chuck, a tenon was turned to fit the opening of the hollow form and its interior was hollowed, all with a spear-point scraper. I was working in tight confines so I needed to work with tools that allowed access to some tricky spaces.

10 Once the tenon size was established, the underside of the lid needed to be shaped so it would sit proud of the vessel. This was done with a finely sharpened finger-shaped spindle gouge. The aim was to leave the smoothest possible surface, reducing sanding to a minimum, and not eliminate the sharp V-groove cut between the tenon and its intersecting surface. I like to separate planes with cleanly cut definition lines.

11 Once sanded, the top needed attention.

12 Parted free, the lid was remounted into a jam-fit chuck turned from the stub left in the scroll chuck.

13 Fitted into place, the top was now ready for shaping.

14 The top was turned to a slightly domed form and sanded through to 320 grit. A fine definition line was cut with a spear-point scraper to create a border and, in effect, a 'frame' to capture the viewer's eye inside the outer perimeter of the lid. I find this most important when I use highly figured timber for lids. I used the same scraper to mark the centre of the lid so I could later drill a hole to accept a delicate finial. This hole can be drilled using the tailstock or a pedestal drill.

15 I like to add finials to my lids to give the overall piece a vertical feel, adding height to the form. To make the finial I grip the wood in a scroll chuck, turning it as finely as possible with a skew chisel and then refining the tapered shape with coarse – 120-grit – sandpaper. Once satisfied with the shape, I cut the tenon with a parting tool, making sure its diameter matches the hole I drilled in the lid. A couple of neatly cut V-grooves add definition to the finial and create a visual break.

16 Part the finial off using a skew so you have a neat tenon.

17 Test to see how the two parts fit, and whether you need something to separate them, as was the case on this occasion.

18 As the lid and finial were fairly similar in colour, I felt a contrasting bead was needed, so back to the scroll chuck. A hole was drilled to accept the finial. Again, a spear-point scraper was used to create a recess into which I could drill. It's not the best way of drilling but it's quick and effective – I hold the drill bit with a pair of pliers.

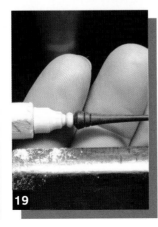

19 Turn the bead, check the size in relation to the finial, cut a tenon at the base and fit the finial and bead to the lid; then you're ready to apply a finish. If you find the bead doesn't do its job, you can remove it or turn another one that does.

SUSPENDED BOX

Curves are the basic shapes of woodturning, and this piece by Joe Winter takes its inspiration from the rounded designs and forms of Luigi Colani, the German industrial designer famous for many years for his biologically inspired designs.

WHAT YOU NEED

- Masur birch, 6¼ × 5⅛ × 4⅜in (160 × 130 × 110mm)
- Cherry or other inexpensive hardwood, 5⅛ × 4⅜ × ¾in long (130 × 110 × 20mm long)
- African blackwood, 3⅛ × 3⅛ × ⅝in (80 × 80 × 15mm) and 3⅛ × ⅝ x ⅝in (80 × 15 × 15mm)
- ½in (13mm) bowl gouge
- ⅝in (16mm) shank swan-neck tipped hollowing tool
- ⅝in (16mm) shank tapered straight-tipped hollowing tool
- ⅛in (3mm) parting tool
- 4½in (115mm) angle grinder
- Home-made 'woodpecker beak' tool (tapered bar with a small, adjustable scraping plate)
- Home-made wooden chuck
- M10 threaded rod
- M33 aluminium thread
- Drill with sanding arbor and extension bar
- Bandsaw
- Abrasives from 120 to 400 grit
- Danish oil, or finish of your choice

INTRODUCTION

Among the new designs in my sketchbook I found that a form I had labelled 'Cyclops' offered a good base design to develop a new shape I had in mind. After some more sketches and modifications I settled on the design I was looking for: a box freely suspended on one side, with an elegant outline that continued from the topside to the base and back. Bowl and stand are made in one piece. I gave it the name 'Jolani'. Now I had to work out how to turn it.

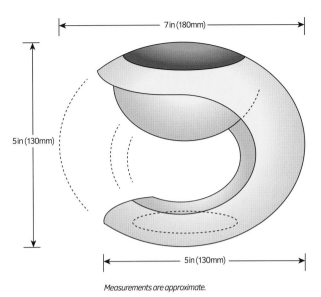

7in (180mm)

5in (130mm)

5in (130mm)

Measurements are approximate.

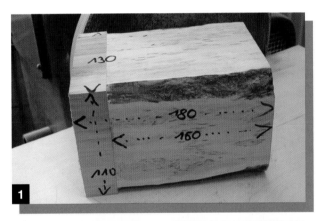

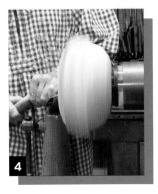

1 I used a piece of masur birch (*Betula pendula* var. *carelica*), but any close-grained, dense hardwood will do. As masur birch is very expensive, I glued on a piece of cherry (*Prunus* spp.) for the part that will eventually be cut away. This must be glued very securely. I prefer the dimensions shown here, but please don't be afraid to change these as you see fit.

2 Mount the wood between centres so the grain is running crosswise, at right angles to the lathe axis. Mount in the absolute centre of the wood. Using a parting tool, turn a recess of 2⅜in (60mm) diameter, or of a size to suit your chuck jaws. Make sure this is of adequate form and size to give a secure hold. Remove the blank from the lathe and reverse it.

3 Draw the profile of the stand on one side of the blank. This will allow you to imagine the end shape better. Cut another recess on the new face and, using the bowl gouge, start to shape the stand, working to the rough outline you have drawn.

4 Using the two chucking recesses, the work can be turned around and rechucked as necessary to allow you to get a better idea of the resulting shape as you work on the upper and lower sides.

5 It is important to achieve a nice rounded shape with identical upper and lower sides.

6 Once you're content with the shape you can sand the outside. I use a 4½in (115mm) angle grinder at 3,000rpm for this step, used with a hook-and-loop sanding pad. Whatever method you use, check at every grit grade used to ensure you achieve the desired surface. Maintain the centres of both recesses for as long as possible; this will give you the ability to re-centre the project when needed.

7 Now to start what I call the PEP turning method, which is turning through the foot. Use any turning tool you choose. I use my own specially designed 'woodpecker beak' tool. This is a tapered bar with a little scraping plate, which automatically slants downwards. To reach every corner you must be able to move the cutter to the left and to the right.

8 Now for hollowing through the foot. Not all lathes have a movable headstock, which may be a little tricky for this project, so get in a comfortable turning position and make gentle cuts to shape the inner section to the form required.

9 Working at the end of the lathe and with the tool of your choice, hollow the piece to half the final depth, in this case about 2⅜in (60mm). The remaining part will become the underside of the box. To be precise, I use two different bars for the hollowing – a straight one and a cranked one – but it is possible to turn with only the straight one, which is the 'woodpecker beak' tool. You can adjust the cutter to the left and right up to about 90°. With the cranked tool, you can reach further around the form a bit more easily.

10 You now need to keep making ever deeper, gentle cuts.

11 Remember to turn the cutter on the tool a little bit to the left as you hollow in the direction of the upper part of the flat area. Keep an eye on the thickness of the foot.

12 The shavings will collect in the interior of the form. Stop hollowing at regular intervals, clean out the shavings and then continue hollowing.

13 Eventually you will find that as the internal shape progresses, you will cut through the square-faced side wall, so at this point a hole appears in the form. As this becomes bigger, the shavings will exit through the hole. Only long shavings will get caught at the rim; remove these, as you need to have a clear sight of the shape you are creating.

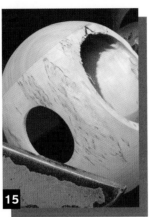

14 Place a light next to the lathe and shine this through the form. This will show you exactly where you need to turn, how and where the tool works and how thick the wall is. It is very useful to be able to see the cut, the shavings and the edge of the piece. Remember to keep adjusting the cutter to reach each area properly. Visualize the interior form and note the need for a round bottom section which will form the underside of the suspended bowl. Form this using the straight hollowing tool.

15 Take care to achieve a consistent thickness, as the outside must be able to withstand a bit of pressure from the self-made chuck. You can see the wood thickness in the shadow.

16 For the hollowing of the box itself, I developed a home-made drawbar chuck. The workpiece is pressed against the wooden chuck through the foot opening, and the pressure of the little cup against the bottom of the box stabilizes it while the top opening is turned.

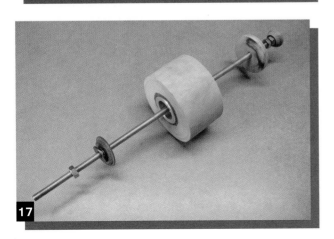

17 The chuck consists of an M10 threaded rod which must be about 4in (100mm) longer than the headstock spindle hole plus the length of the wooden chuck, which has a plain-drilled hole on its underside; I drill out a hole and glue an M33 aluminium thread in place to secure it to the headstock. The pressure plate to secure the foot area is built up with a wooden washer, a steel washer and a nut. The support for the underside of the box is a wooden cup with a thread. This cup is drilled and a nut glued on the underside; once it is in place, you can tighten the nut.

18 The spigot of the wooden chuck must fit exactly to the foot and must be shallower than the thickness of the foot.

19 Put the threaded rod through the headstock spindle and the screwed-on wooden chuck. Attach the workpiece to the chuck through its foot, and place the wooden washer, the nut and the cup inside. At the other end of the spindle place a washer and a nut. Centre the washer and secure the workpiece onto the wooden chuck using both nuts. This will allow the wooden dish section to be placed against the underside of the box. Screw the cup outwards to get good pressure, but be careful not to create too much pressure, or the stand or bowl might develop a crack.

20 You can now turn the interior of the box, but be careful here. For this purpose I use the 'woodpecker' again. Keep the cutter sharp and make light cuts to avoid excess tool chatter.

21 Once the inside is shaped, sanding it should not be a problem. To access the inside easily, use an extension bar in a power drill which has a sanding arbor at the end. The extension bar has a home-made loose-fitting wooden handle which can be gripped to stabilize it.

22 Now to shape the stand. Once you have sanded through the grits, remove the project from the lathe. Use a pair of compasses placed on the centre of the spigot to draw a circle around the lower half of the piece, just touching the outer flat section.

23 Use a bandsaw to cut along this line. Leave the pencil mark in place, and keep the piece stable on the bandsaw. Keep your fingers out of the line of cut and remember to cut slowly.

24 The stand is now starting to take shape.

25 Now chuck the object using the box opening. You need to line the jaws with tissue paper to minimize marking. This works very well with dovetail jaws, because they pull the object towards the chuck. You can now sand the inside.

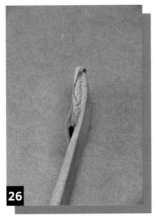

26 This is a specially formed hand-sanding tool for the underside of the form, which uses hook-and-loop-backed abrasive.

27 These are the sanding heads which I made myself with hook-and-loop backing; these help with sanding the inside of the form. Now it is time to sand the rough-cut edges and smooth them off. Check over the piece to make sure it is all finished nicely.

28 I used African blackwood (*Dalbergia melanoxylon*) for the lid. The little brown markings in it match the brown of the body grain very well. The bottom part of the lid is about 3⅛ × 3⅛ × ⅝in (80 × 80 × 15mm), and the finial measures about 3⅛ × ⅝ × ⅝in (80 × 15 × 15mm).

29 Fit the small square section between centres, using pressure to hold the wood against the face of the jaws. Turn the piece to a disc, slightly larger than the eventual required size of the rim, and cut a recess to fit your chuck jaws. Reverse the piece in the chuck and turn the underside of the lid, fitting it to the opening in the box. To reduce weight, you could hollow the inside. Turn an auxiliary wooden spigot fitting exactly to the opening of the hollow form.

30 Now create a waste-wood chuck to accept this spigot.

31 Once the lid is secure, turn the top face of it. As you do so, check the continuity of curves in the body and lid shapes. When you are happy, drill a hole in the centre of the lid, about ¼in (6mm) or so, for the finial. Next, sand the lid and remove the chuck and lid from the lathe.

32 Shape the finial just as you like, and turn a spigot to match the drilled hole in the lid. I like to chamfer the tops of my finials on a sander; then it is time to glue the finial into the lid. For finishing, I use Danish oil on the whole piece, but you can use whichever finish you prefer.

JARRAH BURR BOX

It's difficult to let go of small pieces of treasured timbers, and sometimes even more difficult to find ways of using them. This box by Andrew Potocnik came about as a challenge to convert a small piece of highly figured jarrah burr into a centrepiece that featured a contrasting lid of highly figured eucalyptus burr.

WHAT YOU NEED

- Jarrah burr
- Contrasting-coloured eucalyptus burrs for collar, lid and finial
- Hollowing tool
- Spindle roughing gouge
- ½in (12mm) gouge
- Undercutting scraper
- Skew chisel
- Round-nose scraper

- Parting tool
- Granny-tooth scraper
- Spear- or diamond-point scraper
- Double-sided carpet tape
- Luthier's bending iron (or substitute, such as a soldering iron)
- ¹⁄₁₆in (1.5mm) brad
- Cyanoacrylate (superglue)

INTRODUCTION

A small piece of jarrah (*Eucalyptus marginata*) burr spurred me on to create a lidded form where I constantly questioned how I could use other leftover pieces too good to throw away. As a further challenge, I opted to turn a thin, tapering handle, steam-bent to replicate the curve of the lid's upper surface. To combine the box and lid, I turned a collar of yet another contrasting timber – which presented a couple of small challenges along the way.

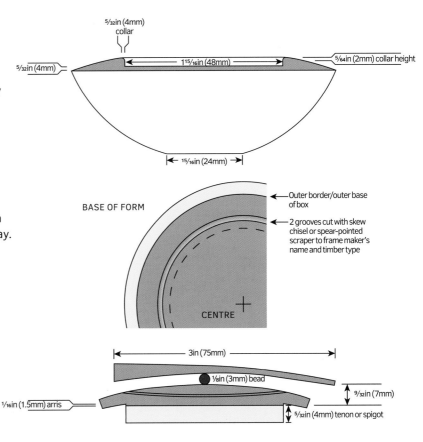

5/32in (4mm) collar

5/32in (4mm)

1 15/16in (48mm)

5/64in (2mm) collar height

15/16in (24mm)

BASE OF FORM

Outer border/outer base of box

2 grooves cut with skew chisel or spear-pointed scraper to frame maker's name and timber type

CENTRE

3in (75mm)

1/8in (3mm) bead

9/32in (7mm)

1/16in (1.5mm) arris

5/32in (4mm) tenon or spigot

1 Saw an offcut of jarrah burr to a neat circle on the bandsaw, for mounting via a three-jaw chuck. Next cut a spigot, ready for the blank to be transferred to a more practical four-jaw scroll chuck. There are lots of other ways you can mount wood on the lathe, but use whatever mechanisms you have, or adopt the techniques you feel most comfortable using.

2 My old three-jaw chuck is welcome at times when I need to hold something large. You could simply turn the blank down between centres to suit any chuck you intend to use, but be sure to cut an angled tenon to ensure maximum grip for your chuck's jaws once the blank is reversed.

3 Turn the basic shape, paying attention to the outer form and the proportions of the inner opening, keeping in mind that a collar will later reduce the opening's size.

4 Use a round-nose scraper to undercut the internal form, or any tools you're more comfortable with. The key here is to open up as much volume inside the container as possible, while not going through the sides.

5 Once the interior is sanded – I work from 120 grit to 180, 240 then 320 grit – it's time to cut a recess that a collar will fit into. I use a 'granny-tooth' scraper for this, but you may find a skew chisel or a parting tool better. The key point is to ensure that the step has neatly cut shoulders and faces, otherwise the collar will not fit correctly.

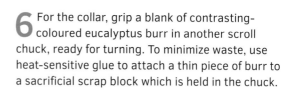

6 For the collar, grip a blank of contrasting-coloured eucalyptus burr in another scroll chuck, ready for turning. To minimize waste, use heat-sensitive glue to attach a thin piece of burr to a sacrificial scrap block which is held in the chuck.

7 Cut a small step into what is to be the underside of the collar, matching the opening you have just cut in the box. Sand as much of the collar as you can. Having parted the ring from its carrier, glue it into position ready for final shaping and sanding. To glue it, I take the work off the lathe, stand the chuck upright and place something heavy on the collar so it sits flat in its recess and bonds tightly.

8 The finished collar stands a little proud of the top of the box.

9 To complete the base, prepare another carrier to match the inner diameter of the collar and apply double-sided tape around the tenon, allowing the box to be remounted in reverse.

10 Turn away the waste wood at the bottom and shape and sand the underside of the piece, with the tailstock supporting the work.

11 With the waste stub sawn away, and relying on the grip of double-sided tape, use one hand to support the box and gently turn away the unwanted wood to create a concave surface. Beware: this is a small piece that requires little trimming, so the tape will suffice, but for anything larger I'd be using an alternative such as heat-sensitive glue or a chuck opened in expansion mode.

12 To make the lid, take another piece of highly figured burr, again attached to a sacrificial carrier. Turn a tenon and undercut what will be the underside of the lid so that it will not sit too high up from the body of the box. Sand the project through to 320 grit and remove from the carrier.

13 Make the carrier into a jam-fit chuck, using Vernier callipers and a granny-tooth scraper to get just the right fit.

14 Press the lid into place to complete the top surface. Cut a fine V-groove about ³⁄₁₆in (5mm) inside the edge to create a border and a visual break in the surface. I used a skew chisel here, but a diamond-point scraper could achieve the same result.

15 To prise the lid out of the carrier, use some padding – in this case, worn-out sandpaper – and a chisel. Work your way around the edge, levering a bit at a time, as the lid is quite thin and brittle.

16 For the handle, turn a piece of dark desert timber so that it flares at the chuck end, almost like a trumpet shape, then sand and cut free. Dome the broad end with a skew chisel and then hand-sand to remove evidence of how it was gripped.

17 After filing and sanding two opposing flatter areas, soak the handle in water and bend to shape using a luthier's bending iron. It's a form of steam bending, and as the heat dries the wood out, it needs to be dipped in water, repeating the process until the wood becomes pliable enough to achieve the curve you're after. I use the heat given off by the iron as it cools to dry the wood. Leaving it just next to the iron, I can get on with the next stage.

18 Turn and sand a small bead; this acts as a spacer between the handle and lid.

19 Use a ¹⁄₁₆in (1.5mm) drill bit, held in a pair of pliers, to pierce a small hole through the bead. You now get an idea of how small the bead is.

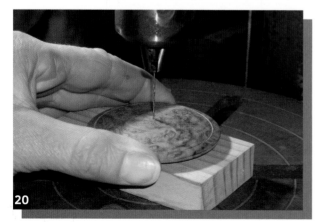

20 Drill a corresponding hole in the lid and handle, and join all three with a ¹⁄₁₆in (1.5mm) brad and cyanoacrylate glue (superglue).

SUGAR BOWL

Every kitchen needs a sugar bowl – ideally one like this one by Mike Mahoney, which will become an heirloom treasured by your family for generations to come. It should have utility and beauty, and be a topic of discussion whenever you have company.

WHAT YOU NEED

- Cottonwood endgrain blank, 6 x 6 x 5in (150 x 150 x 125mm)
- African blackwood, 1⅜in (35mm) square
- Thin parting tool
- Scraper, modified as shown in step 13
- 1¼in (32mm) spindle roughing gouge
- ½in (12mm) bowl gouge
- ½in (12mm) beading/parting tool
- ⅜in (10mm) spindle gouge
- 16tpi thread chaser
- Vernier callipers
- ½in (12mm) twist drill
- Paste wax
- 0000 steel wool
- Oil-based polyurethane
- Foam applicator

INTRODUCTION

For this project you will need a beautiful piece of defect-free, highly figured cottonwood (*Populus fremontii*) or similar timber. This poplar species grows in abundance all over North America. Most craftspeople will not use it because of its abrasive effect on tool steels, and because it is tricky to cut cleanly. However, with all its negative attributes, it is hard to deny its beauty. My sugar bowl will also have an African blackwood (*Dalbergia melanoxylon*) knob that is hand-threaded to the lid. This will contrast nicely with the whitish cottonwood and add special interest to the piece. Whatever woods you use, make sure they are pretty.

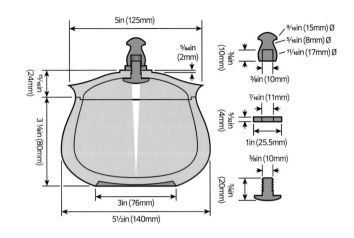

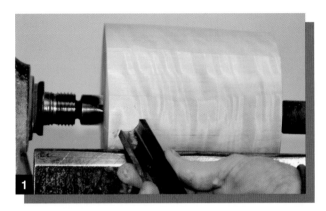

1 Start with a very dry endgrain piece of timber 6 × 6 × 5in (150 × 150 × 125mm), where 6in (150mm) is the diameter of the bowl and 5in (125mm) is the height. Mount between centres with the end grain running parallel to the bed using a spur drive, and round the piece up with a 1¼in (32mm) spindle roughing gouge. Form a 1⅝in (40mm) tenon ⁹⁄₃₂in (7mm) deep at both ends.

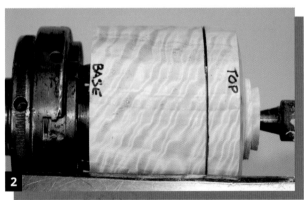

2 Put the base into the chuck and mark where to part the lid, at one-quarter of the length of the piece.

3 Part the lid off with a thin parting tool. Give the box body its rough shape and hollow it, leaving about a ⁹⁄₁₆in (15mm) wall thickness. Leave the project to sit for a day or two; this will help to achieve a better fit between lid and base.

4 Returning to the project, finish-turn the bowl with a ½in (12mm) bowl gouge. Sand the entire piece to 400 grit. Remove the base and measure the interior diameter with Vernier callipers.

5 Mount the lid and transfer the calliper measurement to it so you can cut a tenon to fit the opening in the bowl.

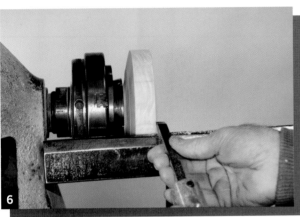

6 Use a ½in (12mm) beading/parting tool to cut this dimension. The tenon will be ³⁄₁₆in (5mm) in depth and should be slightly loose, but not a sloppy fit on the bowl.

7 Use a ⅜in (10mm) spindle gouge to cut a sharp, coved surface with the smallest diameter that will meet perfectly to the body of the bowl. With a ½in (12mm) beading/parting tool, cut a ⁵⁄₆₄in (2mm) groove where the lid will meet the body. This will let you know where the two pieces come together, and it also provides a nice visual break in the coved surface.

8 Finish the interior with a ⅜in (10mm) spindle gouge and drill a ½in (12mm) hole through the centre of the lid. This is where the finial will connect.

9 Make a jam chuck from a piece of green wood; this will hold the lid.

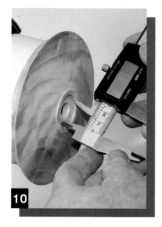

10 Use a ⅜in (10mm) spindle gouge to finish the top of the lid. Form a slightly raised detail that is 1⅝ (40mm) in diameter on the exterior and 1³⁄₁₆in (30mm) on the interior, which is ⁵⁄₆₄in (2mm) deep. This is where the knob washer will sit. Sand the lid to 400 grit, being careful to keep the crisp details.

11 Now make a jam chuck for the body from the same piece of green wood you used to hold the lid. Remove the tenon, shape the foot and sand to 400 grit.

12 For the knob or finial, chuck an endgrain piece of African blackwood 1⅜in (35mm) square. Cut the diameter down with a ½in (12mm) beading/parting tool to 1³⁄₁₆in (30mm). Drill a ½in (12mm) hole in the centre. Sand the face and sides to 600 grit and part the washer off so it will be ⁵⁄₃₂in (4mm) thick. This will sit proud on the top of the lid. To make the knob you need to round the piece to ¾in (20mm) diameter.

13 Drill a ⁵⁄₁₆in (8mm) hole ⅜in (10mm) deep to start the female thread. Cut a relief in the back of the drill hole to provide a place to run the thread out with the modified scraper shown here.

14 Cut a chamfer on the front to get the thread started, then use a 16tpi chaser to accomplish the job.

15 Once you have developed the female thread on the underside of the lid, make a male thread chuck to shape the exterior of the knob – the knob should screw on tightly.

16 Use a ⅜in (10mm) spindle gouge to develop the finished knob, then sand to 600 grit.

17 To make the screw that will hold the knob onto the top, use a 1⅛ × ¾in (30 × 20mm) piece of African blackwood with one-third of its length held in the chuck.

18 Turn the bowl round and measure the interior of the female thread of the knob; it should measure ¹¹⁄₃₂in (9mm).

19 Reduce the diameter to ³⁄₈in (10mm) and cut a stop ⁵⁄₁₆in (8mm) long where the thread will run out. You also need to add a chamfer to start the thread.

20 Develop the thread and check to see if it fits well into the knob. Cut the dowel down behind the thread so it just fits through the washer and lid. This will centre the knob onto the lid when everything is threaded together.

21 The shortened thread should only extend ³⁄₁₆in (5mm) above the washer. Check this by assembling the lid and washer and placing these together over the screw held in the chuck.

22 Flip the screw around in the chuck and secure it by means of the dowel.

23 Part off the excess and make a domed surface with a ½in (12mm) beading-and-parting tool. Sand the domed surface to 600 grit. Now your washer, screw and knob are completed. Finish with a light paste wax to polish each component. Use 0000 steel wool between coats.

24 Assemble all the blackwood parts and then put them together on your sugar bowl, which should be finished with an oil-based polyurethane. Brush on three coats with a foam brush and wipe off each coat with a paper towel so the finish won't build and look like plastic. Use steel wool between coats.

SPINNING TOP BOX

This sophisticated and attractive small box by Bob Chapman has a lid fashioned as a spinning top. A fun feature is that the box has a concave base that is perfect for spinning the top on.

WHAT YOU NEED

- Oak, ¼ × 2¼ × 2⅝in (55 × 55 × 65mm)
- Padauk, ⅜ x ⅜ × 2¼in (10 × 10 × 55mm)
- ½in (13mm) bowl gouge
- ⅜in (10mm) bowl gouge
- ⅜in (10mm) spindle gouge
- 1in (25mm) round-nose scraper

- ⅛in (3mm) parting tool
- Narrow parting tool
- Drill chuck and ¼in (6mm) twist drill
- Diamond hone or whetstone
- Cyanoacrylate (superglue)
- Beeswax and carnauba wax

INTRODUCTION

I have made these for many years and they have proved to be very popular at craft fairs. Careful selection of contrasting woods – in this case oak and padauk – results in a smooth and tactile object, and the grain patterns of the two woods look well together.

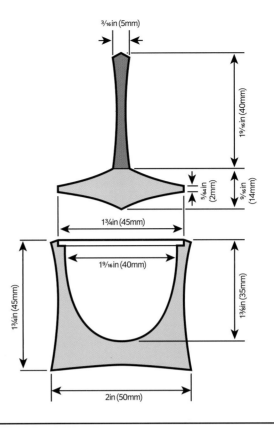

1 The dimensions of this box are not critical and can be varied to suit the timber you might have available. In this instance, the larger block is oak (*Quercus robur*) approximately 2¼ × 2¼ × 2⅝in (55 × 55 × 65mm), and the smaller is Andaman padauk (*Pterocarpus dalbergioides*), ⅜ × ⅜ × 2¼in (10 × 10 × 55mm).

2 It is quite safe to grip a square section like this in a four-jaw chuck, as long as the chuck jaws do not protrude outside the body of the chuck. The square section is turned to the round with a ½in (13mm) bowl gouge, although a spindle roughing gouge could be used just as effectively.

3 The long point of a skew chisel held flat on the rest is ideal for cutting a small, approximately ³⁄₁₆in (5mm) dovetail spigot on the end of the block. This allows the block to be reversed in the chuck and held even more securely for subsequent operations.

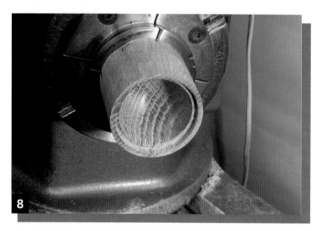

4 After cutting a second ³⁄₁₆in (5mm) dovetail on the other end, a section of the block approximately ⅝in (15mm) long, including the second dovetail, is parted off. This will become the lid of the box. As far as possible, we want to avoid losing the grain match, so use the narrowest parting tool you have; this one is home-made from a machine hacksaw blade.

5 Working about ⅛in (3mm) in from the edge, use an ordinary parting tool to cut a groove approximately ³⁄₁₆in (5mm) deep in the end of the box body blank. Ensure that the sides of the groove are parallel to the lathe axis. The bottom of this groove is the shelf which the lid will sit on. Its width doesn't matter at this stage, as it can be adjusted when the box is hollowed.

6 Use a ⅜in (10mm) spindle gouge to bore a hole in the box and then widen it out towards the edges. The black ink mark on the gouge indicates the required depth of about 1⅜in (35mm). Remember to maintain a curve on the interior of the box, as shown in the drawing.

7 Use a 1in (25mm) round-nose scraper for refining the curve and smoothing the interior. Sharpen the scraper and then hone away the burr using a diamond hone or a whetstone. Arrange the toolrest so that the scraper is perfectly horizontal and its cutting edge is exactly on centre height. Keep the scraper horizontal as you take light cuts until the interior is smooth and nicely curved.

8 Sand the interior, then seal and polish with beeswax and carnauba wax to a soft sheen. Mark the position of chuck jaw number one on the outside, and remove the box body from the chuck. Marking the position of jaw one will allow the box to be replaced in the same position later on.

9 To make the lid, put the lid section in the chuck, gripping it by the dovetail spigot formed earlier. Using a small gouge or even a scraper, shape the underside of the lid to a curve, forming a 'spinning point' in the centre. Sand and polish the pointed surface.

10 Using a freshly sharpened parting tool, reduce the diameter of the lid until it is a tight fit in the box body. Keep bringing up the box body to test the fit and work slowly, removing a little at a time. When a satisfactory fit has been achieved, remove the lid from the chuck.

11 Replace the box body, positioning jaw one with the alignment marks you made earlier. Push the lid into the body and make sure everything turns truly with the lathe on. With a drill chuck in the tailstock, drill a ¼in (6mm) hole about ¼in (6mm) deep into the lid. If the lid isn't tight enough to allow this, use a layer of tissue to tighten the fit until you can work on the lid without it loosening.

12 For the spindle, change the lathe chuck to one with long-nosed jaws to make holding the blank for the spindle easier. If you only have one chuck, you'll have to remove the box and replace it later. Use a parting tool to turn down the end ³⁄₁₆in (5mm) of the spindle until it is a good fit in the hole in the lid.

13 Replace the box in the chuck and use a few drops of cyanoacrylate (superglue) to glue the spindle into the box lid, bringing up the tailstock for support while applying gentle pressure; take care not to overdo it or you risk splitting the spindle. Use a small gouge to shape the top of the lid into the spindle. Finish off with the round-nose scraper, held horizontally on centre, to blend the curve of the lid into the curve of the spindle. Note: the top edge of the box body forms part of this continuous curve.

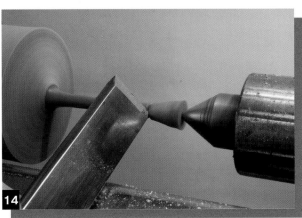

14 Use the long point of a skew chisel to shape the top of the spindle at about 1⁹⁄₁₆in (40mm) from the top of the box. Take care with this cut and remove the tailstock before finally parting off the waste, still using the skew. This should leave a smooth top surface. Complete the sanding, sealing and polishing of the lid. When finished, pull the lid from the box and sand gently around its edge to ease the fit, if necessary.

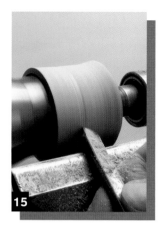

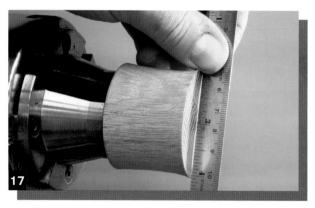

15 Now you need to refine the body. Use the long-nosed jaws to hold the box body, by expanding them inside the opening. If you can't do this, mount a piece of scrap wood and turn a spigot to hold the box body as a tight jam fit. Note the tailstock giving added support. Use a spindle gouge to shape the sides of the box to a gentle concave curve.

16 Finally, remove the tailstock. Very gently, because the box is not held very securely, remove the spigot with a small bowl gouge, taking very light cuts. If you are unsure about doing this, leave the tailstock in place and remove the final small stub with a sharp knife at a later stage.

17 Aim to form a slightly concave base on the box so that it will sit firmly on a flat surface. Sand, seal and polish the whole of the box body.

Note how the lid sits flush with the sides and blends gently into the spindle or finial.

When the box body is turned over, the concave base makes a handy platform to spin the top on.

HANDY HINTS

- Honing the burr from the top surface of a scraper makes it much less aggressive to use and will allow much finer cuts to be made. Keep it horizontal with the cutting edge at centre height and use it with a light touch.

- Loose lids are allowed! Many customers dislike tight-fitting lids: if the lid doesn't come off easily they put the box down for fear of breaking it.

- If you have to allow the chuck jaws to stick out from the chuck body, it is a good idea to wrap a couple of turns of brightly coloured insulating tape around the protruding ends of the chuck jaws. Not only will they help to remind you, but they will also cushion the blow if you forget!

- When parting off a section for a box lid, always use the narrowest parting tool you have available. The less wood you remove in the cut, the better the grain pattern will match from the body into the lid. Ultimately, this will all add to the aesthetics of the final design.

LIDDED FORM WITH FINIAL

This distinctive lidded form by Mark Sanger incorporates a metal bead and a free-form finial. Pieces of this type are normally rough-turned from unseasoned wood and allowed to season fully before finish-turning some months later. However, seasoned wood can be used, as long as a few considerations are taken into account to ensure a good fit to the lid.

WHAT YOU NEED

- Yew blank slightly larger than the box dimensions
- Anjan blank slightly larger than the lid dimensions
- ½in (12mm) bowl gouge
- ⅜in (10mm) spindle gouge
- ½in (12mm) skew chisel
- ¼in (6mm) parting tool
- ⅛in (3mm) parting tool
- 1in (25mm) square-end scraper
- Tipped shear scraper
- Proprietary hollowing tool
- Jacobs chuck with 1in (25mm) sawtooth bit and 2in (50mm) hook-and-loop arbor
- ⅛in (3mm) drill bit
- Depth gauge
- Rule and pencil
- Kitchen towel
- Power drill with 2in (50mm) sanding arbor and hook-and-loop abrasive, 120–400 grit
- Fine-bladed saw
- Chisel, or reciprocal carver
- Vernier callipers
- Abrasive paper, 600 grit
- Cellulose sanding sealer
- Wax finish of your choice
- PVA glue
- Medium-viscosity cyanoacrylate (superglue)
- Soft 8in (200mm) buffing wheel
- Fine-point bradawl
- Large pair of wire cutters
- PPE: Wear latex-type gloves when using superglue

INTRODUCTION

This project uses seasoned yew (*Taxus baccata*) for the main form measuring 8in (200mm) diameter by 6¾in (170mm) in length, with a contrasting wood (anjan, *Hardwickia binata*) for the lid and finial. The form is turned endgrain, with the grain running parallel to the spindle axis of the lathe. Alternatively, a seasoned bowl blank could be used to make a more squat form.

In either instance, due to the addition of a lid, I recommend even with seasoned wood that the form be turned to the finished size, leaving the internal diameter of the neck slightly undersize. Leave the chucking spigot in place and take the piece into your home to settle for a few days before finishing and fitting the lid. Simply removing the material from the inside of the form will allow some movement to occur, and this, though small, can affect the fit of the lid.

For the main form, lid and finial size, I have worked in thirds – for example, the base diameter is one-third of the form diameter and the external diameter of the lid is again one-third of the main form diameter. The finial height (including the bead) is half the height of the form, so that when placed onto the form it becomes one-third of the whole piece. This rule does not have to be rigidly adhered to but it is a good starting place.

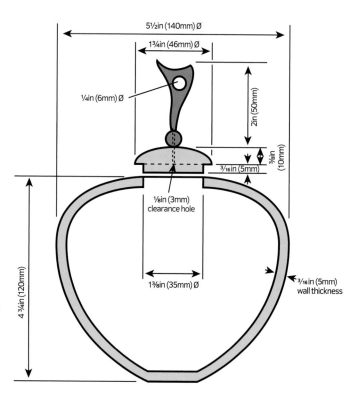

1 First make the hollow form. Mark both ends of the blank and place between centres. Use a ½in (12mm) bowl gouge to rough down to the round, setting a suitable speed for your lathe with regard to the size of the blank used.

2 Use the same bowl gouge to clean up the front face of the blank, turning in towards the revolving centre from the external diameter.

3 Mark on the front face the diameter of the spigot to suit your chuck jaws. Do this with a rule and pencil, with the lathe set to a slow speed.

4 Still using the ½in (12mm) bowl gouge, turn to this line and produce a spigot to the correct length to suit the chuck jaws. True up the spigot using a ½in (12mm) skew chisel held horizontal on the toolrest in a trailing mode.

5 Mark one-third of the way down from the top of the blank; this represents the centre of the shoulder of the form. Turn the profile towards the base from this line.

6 Using the ½in (12mm) bowl gouge, blend from the shoulder towards the headstock. Produce the shape for the upper part of the form, working in towards the drive centre to a safe distance.

7 Reverse the form into the chuck and bring up the revolving centre to centralize the form before tightening the chuck. Use the ½in (12mm) bowl gouge to clean up the front face, and mark the external diameter of the neck using a pencil and rule as before. Turn up to this line, producing a small shoulder of ¹⁄₁₆–¹⁄₈in (2–3mm) in height.

8 Using a 1in (25mm) square-end scraper, scrape the outside profile of the form to remove any tool marks.

9 Using a 1in (25mm) sawtooth bit in a Jacobs chuck, drill out the form to depth. Measure the height of the form and mark this on the bit – minus ³⁄₈in (10mm) – using a marker. Withdraw the bit regularly to remove the shavings and to prevent binding.

10 Begin to hollow the form by opening the entrance hole to the previously marked line. Work from the shoulder down towards the base, and use callipers to measure the wall thickness regularly, aiming for a thickness of ³⁄₁₆–¹⁄₄in (5–6mm).

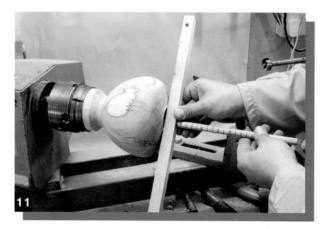

11 Check the depth with a depth gauge before finishing, taking a measurement from inside and comparing this to the outside base line. Then finish with hollowing tools, leaving the base around 5⁄16in (8mm) thick. The base will be concaved slightly later to allow the form to sit properly, thus removing some of this thickness.

12 Using a tipped scraping tool, shear-scrape the inside profile to a good finish.

13 Finish the outside using hook-and-loop abrasive from 120 to 400 grit on a 2in (50mm) sanding arbor in a power drill. Dampen the surface with a small amount of water on a kitchen towel and cut back with 600-grit abrasive once dry.

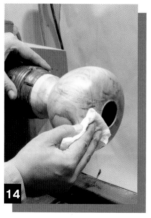

14 Apply several coats of cellulose sanding sealer, removing any excess with kitchen towel. If required, cut back with a 600-grit abrasive by hand. Buff the form, with the lathe speed set to around 1,000rpm, using kitchen towel or safety cloth. Alternatively, the whole form can be buffed using a buffing system when completed.

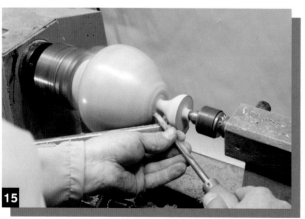

15 Make a friction drive (jam chuck) from waste wood to fit the opening of the form, and set this in the lathe chuck. Protect the form by placing kitchen towel over the drive, and bring up the revolving centre. Using a 3⁄8in (10mm) spindle gouge, refine the base profile and turn down the waste material to a diameter of 3⁄8in (10mm). Concave the base and blend the profile. Clean up with the 1in (25mm) scraper. Finish with 120–600 grit abrasive, apply sanding sealer and buff as before. With the lathe stationary, cut the waste material from the base using a fine saw blade. Remove the remaining waste using a sharp chisel or a reciprocal carver and blend with abrasive. Finish as before with sanding sealer, then apply your chosen wax and buff by hand.

16 Now for the lid. Rough the blank so that the outside diameter is larger than the shoulder of the main form. Turn a spigot on one end to fit the chuck jaws, and tighten into the chuck. Clean up the front face using a ⅜in (10mm) spindle gouge to remove the centre mark.

17 Using Vernier callipers, measure the internal diameter of the opening in the form and transfer this measurement to the front face of the lid blank. Only allow the left tip of the Vernier callipers to contact the wood while trailing the tip.

18 Use a ¼in (6mm) parting tool to part down just short of this line, making the shoulder approximately ³⁄₁₆in (5mm) wide.

19 Offer the form up to the lid and continue to remove small amounts of material with the 1¼in (6mm) parting tool until a good fit is achieved.

20 Measure the outside neck diameter of the hollow form and mark, as before, onto the underside of the lid. Using the ¼in (6mm) parting tool, part down short of this line, making it approximately ³⁄₁₆in (5mm) wide. Offer the form up to the lid and continue to remove small amounts of material until the external diameter of the lid matches that of the neck.

21 Using the ¼in (6mm) parting tool, produce a recess approximately ³⁄₁₆in (5mm) deep by ½in (12mm) diameter in the underside of the lid. Once complete, rotate the parting tool anticlockwise and use it to slightly scrape or round over the edge of the recess.

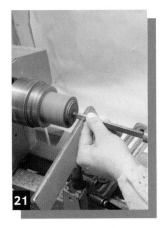

22 Use a ½in (12mm) skew chisel, laid horizontally on the toolrest in trailing mode, to produce a countersink in the centre of the recess to take the head of the wood screw. In this instance the depth will be ¼in (6mm) and the diameter ⅛in (3mm).

23 Using the toe of the skew in a scraping, slightly trailing mode, produce several beads on the underside of the lid.

24 Use a ⅛in (3mm) drill to bore a central hole approximately ¾in (20mm) deep, so that when the lid is parted off the hole will go all the way through.

25 Finish the underside by hand with abrasives from 240 down to 400 grit. Only clean up the outside diameter of the lid lightly with 320–400 grit, regularly checking that the form fits well.

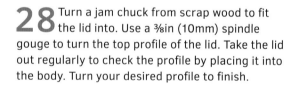

26 Apply cellulose sanding sealer, allow to dry and buff back with kitchen towel with the lathe set to 1,500rpm.

27 Using a ⅛in (3mm) parting tool, part into the lid, leaving it approximately ¾in (20mm) thick to allow for the forming of the top profile. Stop the lathe prior to parting all the way through, and cut off the lid with a fine saw blade.

28 Turn a jam chuck from scrap wood to fit the lid into. Use a ⅜in (10mm) spindle gouge to turn the top profile of the lid. Take the lid out regularly to check the profile by placing it into the body. Turn your desired profile to finish.

29 Once complete, finish to 600 grit as before. Apply sanding sealer and buff with kitchen towel or safety cloth with the lathe speed running around 1,500rpm. At this stage you can apply your chosen wax or other finish, if desired. The lid will eventually be completed with the addition of a small contrasting button on the underside to cover the screw head.

30 Draw the desired finial shape onto a piece of paper and stick this to the wood using PVA glue. Alternatively, the design can be drawn directly onto the wood. Use a scrollsaw, or cut out by hand using a coping saw. Cut slightly outside the line, so the shape can be refined later.

31 Use a suitable diameter drill, in this case ⁵⁄₁₆in (8mm), to drill out the circular opening. A pillar drill can be used if available.

32 Shape and blend the outside of the finial using 120 grit held on a 2in (50mm) hook-and-loop arbor in a Jacobs chuck in the headstock of the lathe. Once the main blending has been achieved, finish by hand using 120 down to 600 grit. Blend the inside of the hole again by hand, either rolling up the abrasive into a tight tube or wrapping it around a small file.

33 Once complete, apply cellulose sanding sealer and buff using a soft 8in (200mm) buffing wheel. Alternatively, buff by hand using a soft cloth when dry.

34 Again using the Jacobs chuck and a small drill, first mark the position for the hole using a fine-point bradawl. Then, using in this case a ⁵⁄₆₄in (2mm) drill, bore a hole ³⁄₁₆in (5mm) deep by holding the finial up to the drill and pushing it onto the bit.

35 Dry-assemble the screw through the base of the lid and the bead. Cut the screw off to length so that around ⁵⁄₃₂in (4mm) is protruding beyond the bead – use a large set of wire cutters for this. Alternatively, cut the screw in a vice with a fine hacksaw. Drip medium-viscosity cyanoacrylate into the hole in the finial and screw the lid, bead and finial together. Align the finial with the grain of the lid, and allow to dry.

36 Turn a small button from alternative material or contrasting wood to fit inside the recess in the underside of the lid and cover the screw. Prepare the button material to fit into the jaws of the chuck. Clean up the front face using a ¼in (6mm) parting tool. Rough down a section of the material and mark the diameter of the recess onto this face with Vernier callipers as before.

37 Using a ¼in (6mm) parting tool, part down to this mark, checking for a good fit into the lid as you proceed.

38 Continue with the same tool, slightly rolling it anticlockwise. Using the burr of the edge as a scraper, slightly dome the front of the button.

39 Measure the depth of the recess and mark this in pencil for the thickness of the button. Part off the button using a ⅛in (3mm) parting tool. Part in until a small amount of material is left, then cut off using a fine saw blade. Place a small piece of abrasive on a flat surface and rub the back of the button flat. Drip a small amount of high-viscosity cyanoacrylate into the recess around the screw head, then push the button into the base. Be careful not to use too much glue, or it can squeeze out and stick to your fingers; in fact, wear latex-type gloves when doing this in case of any overspill. The lid is now fully complete. Apply wax to the lid and finial, then buff by hand.

HANDY HINTS

- If the lid gets stuck in the jam chuck, gently remove it using a screw in the centre hole.

- To achieve a good fit for the lid, finish the form and the lid so the lid fit is slightly tighter than required. Once finished, the entrance hole in the main form can be refined to the exact size of the lid by using 600-grit abrasive inside the hole. All that is needed then is to apply the wax finish to the edge of the opening and finally buff with a cloth.

- Once you have produced a finial shape you are happy with, take a picture of it and use computer photo software to crop it to the exact height and width. This can now be scaled up or down for future use.

- You can make several lids at a time, which can then be used later for similar-sized forms. In this case, turn the hole in the form to fit the lid instead of the other way round.

LIDDED BOX

This piece by Tracy Owen takes its inspiration from the traditional apothecary jar. Made from an unusually spectacular piece of yew, it exploits the contrast between the red-brown heartwood and the pale sapwood.

WHAT YOU NEED

- Yew blank, 6 × 6 × 3½in (150 × 150 × 90mm)
- 1/16in (1.5mm) parting tool
- 3/8in (10mm) spindle gouge
- 1/2in (12mm) spindle gouge
- 1in (25mm) round-nose scraper
- 1¼in (32mm) roughing gouge
- Diamond parting tool
- 3/4in (20mm) skew chisel
- 3/8in (10mm) bowl gouge

- Shear scraper
- Vernier callipers
- Abrasive paper, 180–400 grit
- Drill with sanding arbor and 600-grit abrasive
- Ultrafine abrasive web or 0000 wire wool
- PVA tape
- Acrylic sanding sealer
- Oil finish if desired

INTRODUCTION

This box was made from well-seasoned yew (*Taxus baccata*) with a moisture content of about 10–11 per cent. This is important when making boxes, where the lid must remain a good fit for a long time to come. For this project, it is best to work into the end grain of the wood to ensure that the box retains the right shape.

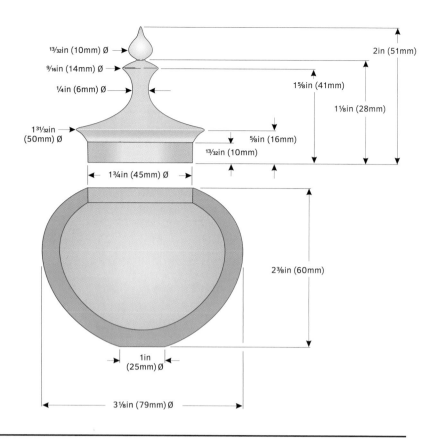

13/32in (10mm) Ø
9/16in (14mm) Ø
1/4in (6mm) Ø
1³¹/₃₂in (50mm) Ø
1¾in (45mm) Ø
2in (51mm)
1⅝in (41mm)
1⅛in (28mm)
⅝in (16mm)
13/32in (10mm)
2⅜in (60mm)
1in (25mm) Ø
3⅛in (79mm) Ø

1 Trim the yew blank to 6in (150mm) long by 3½in (90mm) square and turn it down to a cylinder using a 1¼in (32mm) spindle roughing gouge. The lathe speed should be about 750rpm. Use a diamond parting tool to square off both ends of the blank. Increase lathe speed to 1,000rpm and use a parting tool to cut a tenon at each end as shown. I used the tip of a skew chisel to change the tenons into dovetails. Use callipers or gauges to measure the right size to fit the chuck.

2 Mount the wood in a chuck. I used a ¹/₁₆in (1.5mm) parting tool to part off the lid from the base. Stop a little short of parting all the way through, and stop the lathe to twist the top off by hand. Put the top part to one side for now. Shape the body of the box using a ⅜in (10mm) bowl gouge, with the cuts going from left to right from the largest diameter so you are working downhill to get the cleanest cuts. Lathe speed should be about 1,000rpm.

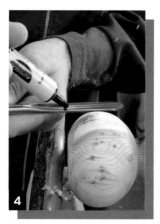

3 Use a 1in (25mm) round-nose scraper held at about 45° to shear-scrape the outside. Pass the tool gently around the piece to follow the shape, again working from left to right from the largest diameter to get the cleanest cuts. Reduce lathe speed to 600rpm.

4 With the outside shaping finished, apart from reducing the base of the box later, it is now time to cut out the inside. A spindle gouge will be used as a drill; use a marker pen to show the depth to stop at. Pick up the cut right on the centre and with the flute facing upwards, and after a few stern pushes, the spindle gouge will act like a drill bit. Keep going until you reach the line from the marker pen.

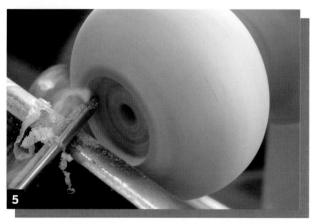

5 Working from the centre outwards, I used a ½in (12mm) spindle gouge, having found that a smaller tool caused too much vibration. At 45°, shear-scrape the inside of the box and the internal edge where the lid will fit. This will leave a fine finish requiring minimal hand-sanding. Sand by hand with 180, 240, 320 and 400 grits, then use an arbor in the drill and power-sand using 600 grit. Lathe speed should be 500rpm. Apply a coat of acrylic sanding sealer and use the handwheel on the back of the lathe to rotate the piece while spraying. Once dry, cut back with ultrafine abrasive web (0000 wire wool will do the same job).

6 I put the body of the box to one side and left it in the chuck it had been worked in. Before mounting the other part of the blank into a different chuck to make the lid-cum-finial, use a ⅜in (10mm) spindle gouge to clean off one face. Lathe speed should be about 1,000rpm. Measure the opening in the top of the box using Vernier callipers and transfer this measurement to the lid blank. Only the left-hand point of the callipers should make contact at this stage.

7 Once the scribed circle lines up with the point on the right, transfer the measurement and make a tenon to fit the base. I used a ⅜in (10mm) spindle gouge to cut back to the scribed line. The body of the box was offered up over the tenon to make sure the fit was right.

8 Cut away the waste before parting off, and undercut the inside of the lid. Hand-sand the faces to fit inside the box and the shoulder using 400 grit. Part off the lid using a ⅟₁₆in (1.5mm) parting tool. Finish the rest of the lid with it fitted into the box body.

9 Start to shape the finial with the tailstock holding the lid in place, then remove the tailstock to do the last few cuts. I made the cuts using a ⅜in (10mm) spindle gouge, working in towards the centre from left and right. Lathe speed was about 750rpm.

10 After sanding, hand-sand the cove of the lid with 180, 240 and 320 grits. Set the lathe speed to 500rpm and use strong PVA tape as extra security to hold the lid, so you can work on the top of the finial without dislodging it from the base.

11 Using the ⅜in (10mm) spindle gouge, make the last few cuts to the tip of the finial, taking great care. My fingers supported the piece to stop it from flexing. Lathe speed was about 750rpm.

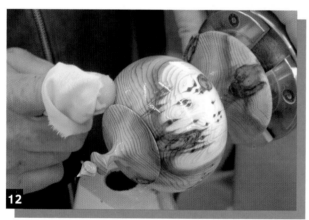

12 Hand-sand the tip of the finial. Remove the tape, spray the lid with acrylic sanding sealer and cut back with abrasive web. If you wish, you could apply a coat of oil on the lathe, using the power of the lathe to buff it to a finish. Part off the base of the box using a ⅟₁₆in (1.5mm) parting tool.

13 For the final cuts on the base, I used the scrap of wood that was left in the chuck to make a jam-fit chuck to hold the body of the box. Leave the tailstock up for the first few cuts, then remove it to finish off. Hand-sand using 240, 320 and 400 grits, oil once more and buff to a finish.

SNOWMAN MONEY BOX

This festive money box by Sue Harker is made from one piece of timber and would make a perfect gift for a child. It can also be made in a decorative version, which would make a lovely seasonal ornament.

WHAT YOU NEED

- Sycamore blank, 4½ x 4½ x 9in (115 × 115 x 230mm)
- 4 offcuts of timber, approximately ⁹⁄₁₆ × ⁹⁄₁₆ × 4in (15 × 15 × 100mm)
- Rubber grommet, 1¾ × ½in (45 × 13mm)
- ½in (12mm) skew chisel
- Swivel-tip scraper
- ⅛in (3mm) parting tool
- ½in (12mm) fingernail-profile spindle gouge
- ⅜in (10mm) fingernail-profile spindle gouge
- Spindle roughing gouge
- Jacobs chuck and drill bit
- Drill and precision drilling jig
- Pillar drill and ³⁄₁₆in (5mm) brad-point bit
- 1³⁄₁₆in (30mm) Forstner bit and extension bar
- Rotary tool with side-milling bit
- Flat file
- Junior hacksaw
- Sanding mandrel and abrasive disc
- Abrasives, 120–400 grit
- Masking tape
- Black and orange acrylic paints
- Pearlescent white acrylic paint (for decorated version)
- Acrylic sanding sealer
- Clear acrylic gloss lacquer
- Cyanoacrylate (superglue)
- Oil finish

INTRODUCTION

The money box is made from a single piece of European sycamore (*Acer pseudoplatanus*), with the main body hollowed out to an even wall thickness. A slot in the hat and a hole drilled through both head and hat allow coins to pass through into the body. A rubber electrical grommet is used to plug the access hole used for hollowing.

The decorative version is left solid and the hat is made from a separate piece of timber so it can be mounted at an angle. The pearlescent white acrylic paint allows the grain pattern to show through while still giving an all-over colour. Of course, this decorated version could be hollowed and made into a money box should you wish – the choice is yours.

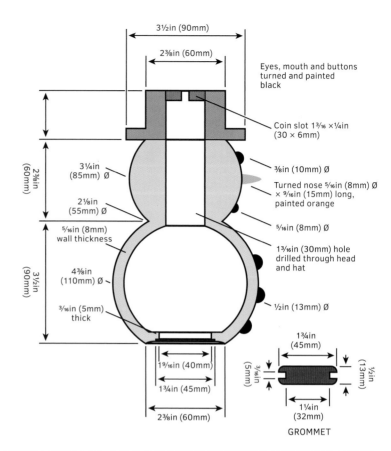

3½in (90mm)

2⅜in (60mm)

Eyes, mouth and buttons turned and painted black

Coin slot 1³⁄₁₆ ×¼in (30 × 6mm)

⅜in (10mm) Ø

Turned nose ⁵⁄₁₆in (8mm) Ø × ⁹⁄₁₆in (15mm) long, painted orange

⁵⁄₁₆in (8mm) Ø

1³⁄₁₆in (30mm) hole drilled through head and hat

½in (13mm) Ø

2⅜in (60mm)

3½in (90mm)

3¼in (85mm) Ø

2⅛in (55mm) Ø

⁵⁄₁₆in (8mm) wall thickness

4⅜in (110mm) Ø

³⁄₁₆in (5mm) thick

1⁹⁄₁₆in (40mm)

1¾in (45mm)

2⅜in (60mm)

1¾in (45mm)

³⁄₁₆in (5mm)

½in (13mm)

1¼in (32mm)

GROMMET

1 Mount the sycamore blank between centres and turn into the round. Next, cut a chucking spigot, the correct size to fit your chuck jaws, at one end of the blank.

2 Now mount the blank in your chuck jaws and bring the tailstock up for added support. Make a pencil mark 3½in (90mm) in from the tailstock; this is the length of the snowman's body. Draw another pencil line at 1¾in (45mm) from the tailstock; this will be the widest part of the snowman. Using a fingernail-profile spindle gouge, form the body into a flat-bottomed sphere.

3 Using a Jacobs chuck with a drill bit fitted, drill to the required depth for hollowing.

4 Cut a recess at 1⁹⁄₁₆in (40mm) diameter and undercut the base deeply enough for a rubber grommet to fit into it. Hollow the body to approximately ⁵⁄₁₆in (8mm) wall thickness. For this I used a swivel tip with a scraper tip attached.

5 Use a skew chisel to refine the opening and cut a recess approximately 1¾in (45mm) diameter for the outer surface of the grommet to sit in.

6 Check the grommet for fit and adjust the opening if required. Make sure the grommet does not sit proud of the base; holding the edge of a ruler across the base is a good way to check this. Sand the body to a finish, starting with 120-grit abrasive and working through 180, 240, 320 and finishing with 400.

7 Mark where the head and hat will start and end. Use a fingernail-profile spindle gouge to shape the head.

8 Turn the shape of the hat. Using a skew chisel, undercut where the rim meets the head and make a crisp cut for the top of the rim. Sand to a finish using the same grits as before.

9 Wrap masking tape around the head and paint the hat with black acrylic.

10 Mark the approximate positions of the mouth, eyes, nose and buttons. Set up a precision drilling jig and drill ¼in (6mm) diameter holes. Try not to drill through into the hollow body.

11 Using a 1³⁄₁₆in (30mm) diameter Forstner bit, attached to an extension bar, drill a hole approximately 6⅞in (175mm) deep through into the head and hat. Wrap a piece of tape round the extension bar to act as a depth gauge. This leaves approximately ⁵⁄₁₆in (8mm) wall thickness at the top of the hat for the coin slot to be cut into.

12 Make a jam chuck for the base of the snowman to fit onto. Bring up the tailstock for support and reduce the diameter of the spigot, finishing the top of the hat as you progress.

13 Instead of parting all the way through, leave a pip of timber, stop the lathe and cut off with a hacksaw.

14 Fit a sanding mandrel into the chuck and attach an abrasive disc. Sand the sawn surface and, working through the grits, smooth the top of the hat to a suitable finish.

15 Mark the centre of the hat and draw a line 1³⁄₁₆in (30mm) long for the money slot. Using a ³⁄₁₆in (5mm) brad-point bit fitted into a pillar drill, bore several holes along the pencil line.

16 With a side-milling bit fitted into a rotary tool, join the drill holes and tidy the slot. Use a flat file to smooth the surface of the slot, and sand to the desired finish using abrasives. Coat the top of the hat and the inside of the slot with black paint.

17 Coat the hole piece with acrylic sanding sealer to seal the surface, before applying several thin coats of acrylic gloss lacquer.

18 While the lacquer is drying, turn the eyes, nose, mouth and buttons. For the eyes, mount a length of timber in the chuck and turn into the round. Mark the spigot length and the diameter of the eye with pencil lines.

19 Reduce the spigot to ¼in (6mm) diameter and turn a ³⁄₈in (10mm) diameter half-bead. Sand the half-bead to the required finish and apply black acrylic paint before parting off. The remaining pieces are turned the same way. The nose and mouth pieces require ⁵⁄₁₆in (8mm) diameter timber, and ½in (12mm) stuff is needed for the buttons. Apply orange paint to the nose. To finish the snowman, apply cyanoacrylate adhesive to the facial features, glue the buttons in place and apply a coat of finishing oil. The festive snowman money box is now complete.

JAPANESE-INSPIRED JEWELLERY BOX

The Japanese design tradition is rich in simple forms, but shows a great ability to transform an everyday utility item into an object of aesthetic beauty. In this project by Mark Sanger, one basic design is treated in two quite different ways: a version with beaded detail and another which is lacquered with applied surface decoration.

WHAT YOU NEED

- Beech blank, 4 × 4 × 4¼in (100 x 100 x 110mm)
- 1in (25mm) spindle roughing gouge
- ⅜in (10mm) spindle gouge
- ¼in (6mm) spindle gouge
- ½in (12mm) skew chisel
- ¼in (6mm) parting tool
- ⅛in (3mm) parting tool
- 1in (25mm) round-nose scraper
- ¼in (6mm) point tool
- Fine-bladed saw

- 1in (25mm) sanding arbor, if available
- Masking tape
- Abrasive, 120–400 grit
- Acrylic sanding sealer
- 0000 wire wool
- Spray acrylic satin lacquer
- Burnishing cream
- Kitchen towel
- Artist's paintbrush
- Gold leaf paint

INTRODUCTION

This simple box in beech (*Fagus sylvatica*) is inspired by a Japanese tea caddy. These are used predominantly today within the tea ceremony and are produced in many simple and elaborate forms. The caddies can retain the natural beauty of the wood, or be highly lacquered and embellished with symbols, such as the crane or, as in this case, a cherry blossom decoration.

The first version shown here has a simple beaded profile, which is intended to hide the join of the lid. The second box is made in exactly the same way, but the exterior is sprayed to give the appearance of a faux lacquer. The traditional method of lacquering is very involved and highly skilled, but a good effect can be achieved using acrylic car sprays, if you adhere strictly to a few rules.

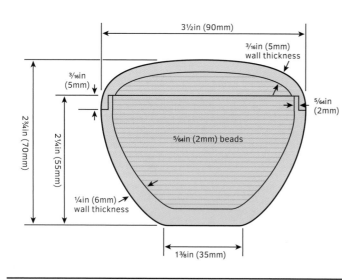

1 Take a parallel-sided beech blank that measures 4in (100mm) square by 4¼in (110mm) long, place it between centres and rough down to round.

2 Using a ¼in (6mm) parting tool, parallel both faces and produce a spigot to suit your chuck jaws. If required, refine the profile of this with a skew held horizontally on the toolrest in the railing mode.

3 With a pencil, mark the position where the lid joins the base – this is approximately one third down from the top face of the blank.

4 Profile the outside shape of the box using a ⅜in (10mm) spindle gouge.

5 Refine the finish you have achieved with a ½in (12mm) skew chisel.

6 Part in with a ¼in (6mm) parting tool centrally over the pencil mark to a depth of ⅛in or so (4mm). Open this out to a width of approximately ⁵⁄₁₆in (8mm) by removing material equally from both sides of the groove; this surface will form the spigot onto which the lid will fit.

7 Placing a ⅛in (3mm) parting tool within this groove, part in towards the lid end, leaving about ¹⁄₆₄in (0.5mm) of the parted groove on the face of the lid – this will be the register line that is opened up to fit over the body spigot.

8 Part in further with the ⅛in (3mm) parting tool to leave approximately ⅜in (10mm) of material. Stop the lathe and use a saw to cut the lid from the base.

9 Using a ⅜in (10mm) spindle gouge, hollow out the inside of the box, leaving the wall thickness around ¼in (6mm), and remembering not to remove the box spigot previously made with the parting tool. In this instance, the internal profile of the box body is curved to match the outside.

10 Using a 1in (25mm) round-nose scraper, refine the inside profile. Make sure the tool is trailing.

11 Finish the inside with abrasive from 120 to 400 grit, either by hand or by power using a 1in (25mm) sanding arbor.

12 Finish the front face and the spigot for the lid down to 400 grit by hand, being careful not to alter the profile of the spigot. Next, seal the inside of the box with acrylic sanding sealer. Allow to dry, then cut back the surface using 0000 wire wool with the lathe running at around 500rpm. Finally, apply several coats of spray acrylic satin lacquer to the inside. Allow to dry and cut back to smooth, as before, with fresh 0000 wire wool – this will give a protective satin sheen to the box's interior.

13 Reverse the lid into the chuck and use a ⅜in (10mm) spindle gouge to profile the inside, stopping short of the registration material left when you parted off.

14 Use a ½in (12mm) skew chisel, held horizontally and trailing on the toolrest, to slowly open out the internal shoulder. Slightly taper this inward, and regularly check the fit with the base. Once the base starts to fit into the lid, gently parallel the internal shoulder until you get a tight fit. Finish this off gently with 320-grit abrasive.

15 Use a 1in (25mm) round-nose scraper to refine the lid interior. Finish by hand down to 400-grit abrasive, but be careful not to abrade the internal shoulder. Apply acrylic sanding sealer and lacquer to finish. Place the body of the box back into the chuck and fit the lid, bringing up the tail centre. Using a ¼in (6mm) spindle gouge, profile the remainder of the top and refine the base. Leave around ⅜in (10mm) at the tailstock end.

16 Use a ¼in (6mm) point tool to produce ⁵⁄₆₄in (2mm) beads all over the box. Use the tip of the tool at the join line to ensure the join is hidden within the base of one side of the bead. Finish the beads by hand.

17 Use a fine saw blade to remove the waste material from the top of the lid. Tape the lid to the base with masking tape and refine the profile with a ¼in (6mm) spindle gouge. Continue the beads to the centre of the lid with the ¼in (6mm) point tool. Remove the masking tape and finish the beads by hand, then apply spray acrylic sanding sealer and allow to dry. Cut back with 0000 wire wool and apply 2–3 coats of spray acrylic satin lacquer, cutting back between coats.

18 Use burnishing cream on kitchen towel to produce a highly finished piece. Set your lathe speed to around 300rpm. Use a clean piece of towel to polish the outside, check the finish, then continue until you achieve the desired gloss.

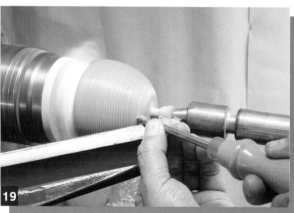

19 Make a jam chuck out of scrap wood to fit the body of the box. Place the body over this and bring the tail centre up. Remove the waste down to around ¼in (6mm) on the base and produce a concave profile so the box will sit properly. Continue the beads around into the base using the ¼in (6mm) point tool as before.

20 Cut the remaining waste from the base using a fine saw blade while holding the base onto the jam chuck. Refine the base with a ¼in (6mm) spindle gouge. Finish the base and beads by hand with abrasive down to 400 grit. Apply acrylic sanding sealer and lacquer, then burnish.

21 The second box is made in exactly the same way as the first, only without the beads. To prepare for spraying, place masking tape around the spigot that fits inside the lid, and fit the base onto a friction chuck (jam chuck) made from waste wood. Finish the base down to 400 grit and apply spray acrylic sanding sealer. As before, cut this back to smooth using 0000 wire wool. Use acrylic deep red car spray to coat the box. Apply fine coats and allow each one to dry.

22 To speed up the drying process, use a hair dryer on the cool setting. Do not try to rush by using hot air, or the acrylic spray will bubble. Once dry, gently rub back the paint to smooth using 320-grit abrasive. Then set the lathe to around 300rpm and use 0000 wire wool to refine the surface further. Keep applying the paint in fine layers, allow to dry and cut back with the wire wool until you have a good coverage and a fine, smooth surface. Your patience and attention to detail here will dictate the quality of the final finish.

23 Once fully dry, affix a copy of the design on page 94 to the box using masking tape.

24 Using a ballpoint pen, carefully draw over your design.

25 Remove the masking tape and drawing – an impression will be left in the paint surface. Use a fine paintbrush and gold leaf paint to fill in this impression. Take your time here.

26 Place on a jam chuck and apply several coats of acrylic satin lacquer. Cut back with wire wool to smooth, then burnish – as you did the uncoloured box – using burnishing cream. Be careful not to cut back too hard, or you may start to remove the gold detailing. With the lathe stationary, buff gently by hand with a soft cloth.

HYBRID BOX

Inspired by the wide range of techniques used in modern woodworking, this box by Andrew Potocnik combines ideas from different disciplines to arrive at something original. But a lot of thought was needed to convert the idea in the maker's mind into a practical finished product.

WHAT YOU NEED

- 2 blanks of red gum or other hardwood to give finished sizes of 4½in (115mm) diameter × 1⅛in (30mm) and 4½in (115mm) diameter × ¾in (19mm)
- Round-nose scraper
- French-curve scraper
- Dome-end scraper
- Granny-tooth scraper
- V-point scraper

- ½in (12mm) bowl gouge
- Rotary tool with burrs, preferably with flexible drive
- Brass wire brush
- Danish oil or polyurethane finish
- Acrylic paints
- Artist's broad brush
- Natural sponge

INTRODUCTION

Returning from a collaborative event several years ago, impressed by the varied techniques I had witnessed there, I engraved, turned and painted until I felt I had combined other people's techniques into something of my own, resulting in my 'hybrid bowl' series. In due course a new development dawned on me: converting the bowl into a hybrid box.

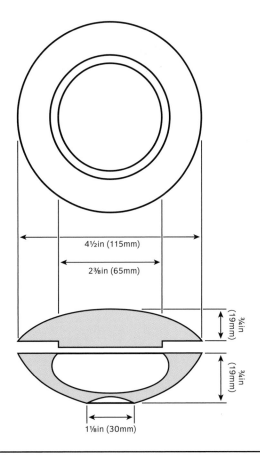

4½in (115mm)

2⅜in (65mm)

¾in (19mm)

¾in (19mm)

1⅛in (30mm)

1 First, take two bandsawn blanks; I used red gum (*Eucalyptus camaldulensis*), a medium-dense hardwood with interlocked grain. Press the first blank against a scroll chuck, using the tailstock to hold it secure so it can be roughed down. In effect, this is a pressure chuck, but the jaws of the chuck need to be extended as far as they can be to spread the pressure over the blank. The tailstock has to be absolutely secure with no creep along the bed, or the holding pressure will fail.

2 Turn a spigot on the tailstock end of the blank, then remove it from the lathe. Reverse it and grip the spigot in your scroll chuck while you clean up the exposed face of the blank.

3 Use a pencil to mark out the outer edge of what will be the hollowed-out section. I also like to create a break between the hollowed section and the area that will be decorated by leaving a small, slightly angled band, so the outer edge of this part will need to be marked, too. Once marked out, the initial hollowing can be done with the ½in (12mm) bowl gouge, followed by a round-nose scraper to refine the interior form of the bowl.

4 Once the hollowing has been done, the outer band is defined with a sharp V-groove cut with the long point of a point scraper or a skew chisel. To check the angle quickly, I used the edge of my scraper to ensure the edge of the band sits below the overall outer rim of the bowl. Once happy, sand it and the hollow to a fine finish, being sure to retain the crisp detail – if not, you run the risk of creating forms devoid of definition that simply curve from one plane to another.

5 With dimensions, angles and sanding out of the way, you can begin to add texture to the rim of the box using a rotary burr. I used a ball-end cutter, but by using different shapes of cutter you can create various patterns. I used to use a small hand-held machine but I now have the motor unit suspended with a flex-drive attached, so it is lighter and easier to manipulate. To get rid of the furry frayed bits of wood left by the burr, clean the surface with a brass wire brush.

6 To complete the underside of the box I used a jam chuck. To make one, fit a blank of the same wood as the bottom into a scroll chuck. The jam chuck then becomes the lid of your box. Once the jam-chuck blank is fitted in the chuck, mark the size of the tenon needed – this will eventually be the mating spigot of the box lid – and turn the waste wood away with a gouge, then trim it to the exact diameter using a home-made 'granny-tooth' scraper. The idea is to make the tenon slightly flared so the box can be wedged into place. The key is to not make the base of the tenon so wide that the rim of the bowl cannot push tight against its base and, in turn, run truly.

7 Use a bowl gouge to remove the bulk of the waste timber and clean up the outer edges of both the bowl blank and the jam chuck. You can bring up the tailstock for support for this part.

8 Use a bowl gouge to shape the bowl's exterior and remove the spigot. Refine the form with a scraper until it sweeps from the edge down to a base of about 1⅛in (30mm) diameter.

9 Where the spigot used to be, create a slight hollow and use a scraper to refine it.

10 Incise a V-cut about one-third of the way down the outside curve. Use a V-shaped scraper to cut it. This defines the area of the carved pattern.

11 Now use the rotary carving tool to carve a similar pattern to that on the top face. When completed, gently lever it free of the carrier with a chisel, inserting some padding so the tool will not mark the finished surface. Then sand and clean up the piece and gently lever it off the jam chuck.

12 Now use a bowl gouge to shape the meeting face of the lid. Don't remove the tenon previously cut for the jam fit; instead, refine it with a point tool and create a hollow, as you did with the base form earlier. After shaping the hollow, cut a couple of V-grooves for decoration. Don't be scared to make these grooves bold, otherwise they'll just look like scratched afterthoughts and will serve little purpose.

13 Sand the top face, hollow the spigot and then carve the outer rim of the lid.

14 Now you can reverse-chuck the lid by holding it in a jam chuck or in a set of jaws, but don't grip too tightly or you will mar the spigot. Bring the tailstock up for support, then turn the bulk of the timber away and rough-shape the lid.

15 Now refine the top shape of the lid. Remove the tailstock and use a scraper to finish the curve and add a V-groove – again, marking the point to which the carving will go. After this you can sand down to 320 grit. Some feel they should sand well beyond this grit, but unless you're working with incredibly dense timbers from arid areas of the world, you shouldn't bother. Bottom line: check the surface of your wood and decide whether you need to go finer.

16 Now carve the piece up to the incised V-cut.

17 Use a brass wire brush to clean up the fuzzy edges of the carved detail.

18 You now need to apply a finish. I normally use a tung-oil-based product such as a Danish oil, but here is an example where I have used a polyurethane-based product. I like the patterned effect. You can alter this piece further by applying some colour if you wish.

19 Once the finish is fully dry you can set about applying colour. I used good-quality acrylic paints that work very well on wooden surfaces, but experiment with what's available in your neck of the woods. I continue to explore those that suit me. To apply paint I used a flat, broad brush followed by a sea sponge. Both should be available in local art supply shops.

20 Painting the textured surface begins with laying down a base colour with a brush. I find it's best to begin with the darkest hue before working through to the lightest, which you'll apply last of all.

21 Dapple the next colour on using a piece of sea sponge.

22 Follow this with another, lighter hue of whichever colour you choose.

23 The final application of paint accentuates the high spots of the textured wood. Using my finger, I like to apply an iridescent paint to protruding surfaces of the carving which, in effect, takes the embellished surface back to where it all began: the carved pattern.

TRIO OF NESTING BOXES

This set of three boxes by Nick Arnull is an abstract take on the familiar Russian doll nesting boxes. Instead of bright paintwork, these boxes have raised panels and carved decoration to add interest.

WHAT YOU NEED

- Three sycamore blanks, approx. 4½ × 4½ × 8in (115 × 115 × 200mm), 3½ × 3½ × 6in (90 × 90 × 150mm), 3 × 3 × 5in (75 × 75 × 125mm)
- 1⁄16in (1.5mm) superthin parting tool
- ¾in (20mm) box scraper
- Large French-curve bowl scraper
- ¼in (6mm) long-grind bowl gouge
- ¼in (6mm) round skew chisel
- ⅜in (10mm) fingernail spindle gouge
- ¼in (6mm) parting tool
- ¾in (20mm) spindle roughing gouge
- Long-neck mini-grinder with sanding attachment
- Hand and power carving tools
- Home-made sanding sticks
- Acrylic sanding sealer
- Artist's acrylic black gesso paint and brushes
- Acrylic satin lacquer
- 2-part wood bleach

INTRODUCTION

I made these boxes as a set of three, which sit nicely as a group display.

When making the prototype for this project, I realized that if I rotated the top section the piece instantly became more dynamic. Creating the multi-box required considerable attention to the numbers involved if the boxes were to fit inside each other; this proved to be something of a challenge. This is not a particularly quick project as it requires great accuracy. The blanks should ideally be rough-turned to allow the timber to relax and move before final turning.

I started with the largest piece, but in hindsight, I feel it would have been easier to start with the smallest. I used European sycamore (*Acer pseudoplatanus*) from the same board for all the boxes, so they would all have similar grain pattern and colour. The dimensions for the individual boxes as shown in the drawings can be altered to suit the size of blank available.

When working on the boxes, the lids need to be a tight fit, but when these are finished the lids need to be easily removed.

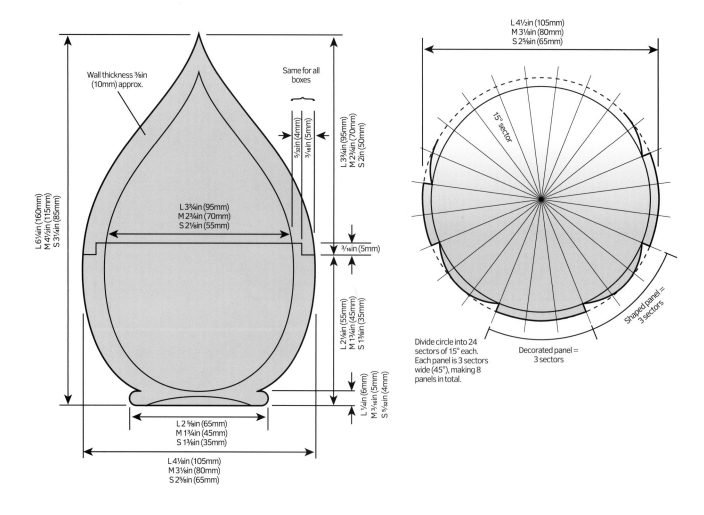

1 Mount the first blank between centres and make round using a large spindle roughing gouge. Create a chucking spigot at both ends of the blank to match your vice jaws, using the ¼in (6mm) parting tool. Mark 1in (25mm) for waste from the left-hand end, followed by the dimensions for the box. You can work this out by dividing the overall length into fifths, then allocating two-fifths and three-fifths for the bottom and the top – this method is used for all the boxes. To achieve a close grain match, use a ⅟₁₆in (1.5mm) superthin parting tool to separate the lid. With the section for the base mounted into the chuck, drill to depth using a spindle gouge, then begin to remove the waste material from the box interior.

2 When the spindle gouge will no longer cope with the overhang, change to a ¼in (6mm) long-grind bowl gouge to complete the hollowing.

3 Finish the inside of the box using a large French-curve scraper.

4 Use a hard-faced sanding block to lightly sand the top face – this will become part of the box opening.

5 Use a ¼in (6mm) parting tool to create the top joint of the box.

6 Sand, seal and finish the inside of the box, then remove from the chuck. Mount the top section of the box into the chuck jaws and drill the centre to the required depth using a ⅜in (10mm) spindle gouge. Then start to open out the inside of the box lid, which will make the next stage easier and allow you clearance as you work.

7 Accurately measure the diameter of the base opening and transfer this to the lid. Ensure this is done accurately, as this forms the joint between box and lid, and needs to be a nice fit to allow the box to be held securely at a later stage.

8 Now remove the rest of the waste material from the inside of the lid, leaving enough room to allow the outside shape to be turned. Consider the shape of the next box that will have to fill the space you have created.

9 Sand, seal and finish the parts completed so far.

10 Return the base to the chuck and fit the lid. True the outside diameter, which needs to be reduced to the final external diameter of the box. At this stage, if you feel the need to use the tailstock for added support, it's not a problem; it also can help when re-centring the box in the chuck jaws.

11 Now remove some of the waste material at the bottom of the box. This will help you to visualize the finished piece.

12 Use the ¾in (20mm) spindle roughing gouge to begin removing the waste wood at the top of the box, and then create the shape required.

13 All this work is carried out using just the roughing gouge. Remove the tailstock at the latter stages to give better access to the point at the top of the box. It feels great to turn such a fine point with a relatively large tool. Use the ¼in (6mm) parting tool to finalize the position of the bead at the base of the box, as well as its diameter.

14 Now finalize the shape at the bottom of the box, blending all the curves together to create a pleasing profile. At this stage, sand the box to a high standard.

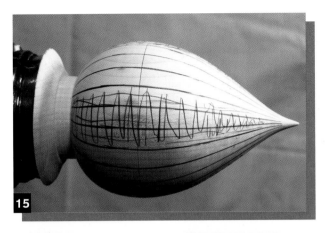

15 Using the indexing head on the lathe, mark out 24 sections equally around the piece, then divide these into four groups, each comprising one shaped and one decorated panel. Define the areas that will become the panels that appear to be raised. When marking out, use a sharp and very soft pencil, such as a watercolour pencil, or the wood will be damaged and this may show afterwards.

16 Use a power carver to carve the boundary lines of the panels, paying careful attention to the points located at the top of the box.

17 Once all the panels have been outlined, the edges need to be raised; this is done with a hand carving gouge. Always work away from yourself and keep your hands behind the cutting edge.

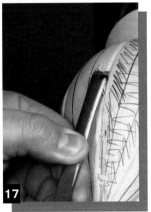

18 Take a hand-held mini-grinder and sand away the excess material to create your desired shape. Here is the grinder with its disc guard in place.

19 Begin to hand-sand the areas between the raised panels – here I used thin bits of wood with abrasive glued to them to allow me into all the areas that require sanding. I will, from time to time, raise the grain using water to lift the fibres, which also helps the final finish.

20 You will need to create a jam chuck from scrap wood, which can be used for the bottom sections of all the boxes. Before mounting the base accurately, measure the final depth of the inner box – you don't want to break through the bottom at this stage. Once mounted into the jam chuck, true the outside of the area that will become the bead at the bottom. Take care not to damage the finished panels.

21 Use a ¼in (6mm) round skew chisel to create a small bead at the bottom of the box – this will give each box a lift and allow it to sit a little higher when placed inside the next larger box.

22 Use the ⅜in (10mm) spindle gouge to dish the underside of the foot. This is an area that is very often given less attention, but it is where every woodturner will look. Therefore, take that extra bit of care and finish it properly.

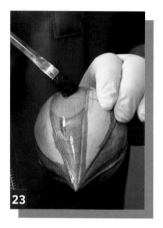

23 Bleaching is just another way to modify the colour of the timber, like liming wax or stain. There are many variations available, so be sure to read the specific instructions for the brand you are using. Here I am bleaching the middle box to achieve the white colour I am looking for.

24 Decorating the dark panels is quite simple and requires only one power tool and some artist's black paint. Acrylic black gesso paint will give a good finish when applied to the panels, and also keeps the risk of colour penetration to a minimum. Use a good-quality flat brush to apply a coat of gesso to the panel, working carefully to avoid over-applying the product. Two coats may well be required.

25 Use a smaller brush to line the edges of the panels, which will make them look much crisper and sharper. Now allow the painted boxes to dry.

26 Use a ball-end cutter fitted into a rotary handpiece to create a random pattern on the black panels. Don't aim for a regular pattern, and definitely avoid creating straight lines.

27 When the box was rotated, I realized that the uncoloured edge would show at the joint, so I added black, using a fine artist's brush, to make the panels appear as if they were set into the box. Don't paint the edges of the white panels, as this would create an undesirable black line at the joint. Spray the finished box with acrylic satin lacquer.

28 For boxes two and three, repeat the process, using the dimensions on the drawing. Here is the finished group of nesting boxes, showing the lids lined up with the bodies.

TUNBRIDGE WARE BOX

Incorporating pictures into turned vessels is very popular today with segmented turners. But it was first made fashionable nearly 200 years ago by the turners of Royal Tunbridge Wells in England and Sorrento in Italy. This box by Dennis Keeling is inspired by this historic technique.

WHAT YOU NEED

- Corian® offcuts: white, granite, black and green
- Hardwood offcut (e.g. mahogany) to form the door
- Tungsten-tipped shear scraper
- Negative-rake side scraper
- Negative-rake flat-ended scraper
- Skew chisel
- Hand plane

- Bandsaw
- Disc sander
- Thick cyanoacrylate (superglue)
- White two-part epoxy glue
- Clamps as needed
- Abrasive discs
- Car-body cutting paste

INTRODUCTION

Tunbridge ware, as it is known today, was crafted by gluing thousands of strips of different-coloured woods together to form a mosaic picture. This is not marquetry using a veneer; it's more like a stick of rock (a boiled-sugar confection traditional at British seaside resorts) with the picture going all the way through the glued-up composite. I thought I would revive this old tradition, but instead of using strips of wood, I would use Corian, a hard plastic material which I had available in many different colours.

A castle motif was widely used by the turners of Tunbridge, as the angular ramparts worked very well with the mosaic pattern.

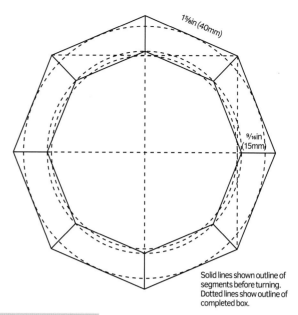

Solid lines shown outline of segments before turning. Dotted lines show outline of completed box.

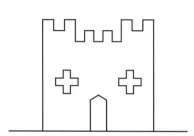

Flat - Corian white	2
Segments	8
Outside diameter	4in (100mm)
Inside diameter	3⅛in (80mm)
Upper wall width	⅜in (10mm)
Lower wall width	⅜in (10mm)
Board thickness	2in (50mm)
Vertical spacers	0in (0mm)
Segment edge length	1⁹⁄₁₆in (41.4mm)
Board width	½in (13mm)
Economy board length	36in (903.1mm)
Mitre angle	22.5°

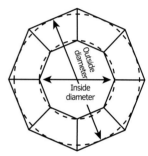

Row	Type	Segments	Board thickness	Outer diameter	Inner diameter	Segment edge length	Vertical spacer width	Board width	Economy board length	Mitre angle
3	Disc Corian white		½in (13mm)	4⅛in (105mm)						
2	Flat Corian white	8	2in (50mm)	4in (100mm)	3¼in (85mm)	1⁹⁄₁₆in (41.4mm)	0in (0mm)	⁷⁄₁₆in (10.7mm)	36in (909.8mm)	22.5°
1	Disc Corian white		⁹⁄₃₂in (6.5mm)	4⅛in (105mm)						

PLANNING THE DESIGN

Sketch the basic castle form and try to recreate it in strips of Corian. This design uses an eight-sided segment ring. I used a CAD package specifically designed for segmented turning to get the dimensions of the segments. The segment size then determines the size of the mosaic composite.

In this case the composite worked out to be 1⅝in (40mm) wide by 2in (50mm) high by 9¾in (250mm) long. This gave enough material to make two round boxes.

1 By trial and error I finally found that ⅛in (3mm) square strips of Corian gave enough mosaic components for the 1⅝in (40mm) segment width. Start by cutting the ½in (13mm) Corian sheet into slabs which measure about 12in (300mm) long. These can then be cut on the bandsaw into ⁵⁄₃₂ × ½in (4 × 13mm) strips. Now cut these strips into ⁵⁄₃₂in (4mm) square lengths. Use white, granite, black and green strips for the design. The door is made from a strip of mahogany (*Khaya ivorensis*); the top of this needs to be hand-planed to form the apex, and you can't plane Corian.

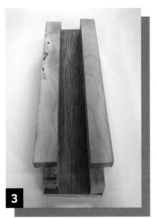

2 Clean up the ⁵⁄₃₂in (4mm) square lengths on the disc sander, bringing them down to approximately ⅛in (3mm) square. They don't have to be very accurate, because any gaps will be filled by glue. You will need over 100 square sections for this design.

3 Construct a wooden trough from scrap timber and line it with polythene sheet; this will enable the mosaic picture to be built up to the full width of the segment, 1⅝in (40mm). Use white Corian strips ¼ × 1⅝in (6.5 x 40mm) for the top and bottom of the segment stack.

4 Gluing each strip separately into a composite proved an impossible task. It is easier to construct sets of glued-up strips. Use four strips side by side for the stonework, with two thin strips of black glued to a wider strip of the same material to form the windows. Glue grey and white strips together to form the battlements. Use a white two-part epoxy glue to simulate mortar in the stonework, and use a clear cyanoacrylate for the black windows.

5 Fix the wooden door centrally to the base piece of white Corian using cyanoacrylate, then add the layers of brickwork using white two-part epoxy. Try to glue up the whole composite in one process – it gets difficult at the halfway mark. Squeeze the segments along their length to ensure the glue is uniform along the length.

6 When the composite has been glued up, add the top strip of ¼ × 1⅝in (6.5 x 40mm) white Corian and clamp the whole composite to get the air bubbles out and to square off the section. It took me four attempts to get this right; the first three versions came out too crooked.

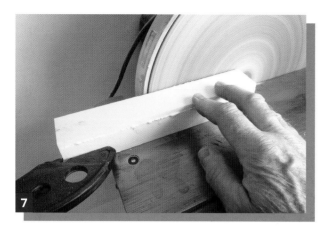

7 After the glue has cured – usually after 24 hours – cut the ends off and clean up the section for cutting. Sand the sides flat on the disc sander ready for cutting the segments on the bandsaw.

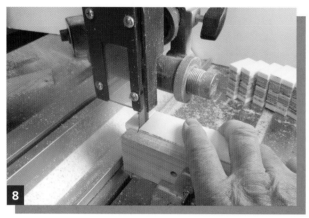

8 Cut the individual segments on the bandsaw; they need to measure ⁹⁄₁₆in (15mm) thick to give plenty of clearance. There should be enough length to get 16 segments from the one composite, which is enough for two boxes.

9 Sand the edges of the segments to the 22.5° mitre angle on the disc sander. Be careful not to sand too much; they should all be roughly the same size. Try to alternate the segment sides for sanding the mitre angle – it makes the box asymmetrical.

10 Before the segments can be glued together it's advisable to prepare the base. Mount a disc of white Corian, ¼in thick by 4½in diameter (6.5 × 110mm), on a wooden faceplate using a paper-glue joint. Pencil a 4in (100mm) diameter ring on the top to show the centre for gluing up the segments of the box body.

11 Dry-mount the segments on the base, using a rubber band, to ensure that they come together as a ring. Any badly fitted joints need to be resanded on the disc sander until they all fit together cleanly.

12 It's easiest to glue the segments to the base and to one another all at the same time. Use white two-part epoxy between the segments and the base. Gently hold them in position using a rubber band. Do not clamp them, otherwise the glue will be squeezed out of the joints.

13 When the glue has cured – usually after about 12 hours – the box body can be mounted on the lathe and the outside turned. Use a tungsten-tipped shear scraper to gently clean up the edges and get the box running true. Have the lathe speed quite slow here – about 500rpm – this will avoid the Corian splintering.

14 Finish the outside with a flat negative-rake scraper. It's only the burr that is cutting, so you need to re-hone the scraper several times to get a good finish.

15 Clean up the inside and bring down to size, initially using the tungsten-tipped shear scraper, then a negative-rake side scraper. Use a skew chisel to clean up the bottom in flat-scraping mode.

16 The lid is made from a disc of ½in (13mm) white Corian 4⅛in (105mm) in diameter. Glue this to a wooden faceplate using a paper joint; this will enable it to be easily separated later. Recess the underside to a depth of about ³⁄₁₆in (5mm) to fit inside the box, using a flat-ended negative-rake scraper. Finally, bring the outside down to the same diameter as the box body.

17 Break the box away from its wooden faceplate and fit it to the top already mounted in the lathe. Hold it in place using a small-toothed centre on the tailstock. Clean up the underside of the box with a flat-ended negative-rake scraper and slightly undercut it to allow it to sit firmly.

18 Bring the outside of the lid down to the same size as the box body using a tungsten-tipped shear scraper.

19 You can now finish the outside of the box, including the lid, using the negative-rake flat-ended scraper.

20 Sand the box using abrasive discs, starting at 120 grit and working up to 1,000 grit. Finally, polish using a car-cutting paste to give a semi-gloss sheen.

JAPANESE-STYLE INRO BOX

Japanese *inro*, invented in the 17th century, are miniature lidded boxes used in place of pockets. By tucking the leather cord and its plain or decorated toggle (*netsuke*) under the belt of the kimono, the boxes could be used to carry small items such as identity seals and medicines. This version by Mark Sanger can be used to store precious things in too.

WHAT YOU NEED

- Ash, 5½ × 2⅜ × 2⅜in (140 x 60 x 60mm)
- Pine, 5½ × 2⅜ × ⅜in (140 x 60 x 10mm)
- Small offcuts of beech and sycamore
- ¾in (19mm) spindle roughing gouge
- ½in (12mm) skew chisel
- ¼in (6mm) spindle gouge
- 1in (25mm) round-nose scraper
- ¼in (6mm) parting tool
- ⅛in (3mm) parting tool
- ¼in (6mm) point tool
- Bench planer
- Bandsaw
- Callipers
- Fine-blade saw
- Knife
- Craft or utility knife blade
- Rotary tool with small round-nose engraving cutter
- ⅛in (3mm) drill
- PVA glue
- Medium-viscosity cyanoacrylate (superglue)
- Abrasive, 120–400 grit
- Spray acrylic sanding sealer
- Spray acrylic black paint
- Spray acrylic satin lacquer
- Masking tape
- PPE: Use lung protection while sanding

INTRODUCTION

The scope for the design is almost limitless, and by including different materials in place of the wooden toggle, beads and leather cord, the design and impact of the box can be greatly altered.

STOCK PREPARATION

For the project I have chosen an ash (*Fraxinus excelsior*) endgrain blank (the grain running parallel to the axis of the lathe spindle), measuring 5½ x 2⅜ x 2⅜in (140 × 60 × 60mm), cut in half lengthways through the middle. The cut faces were then planed flat on a small bench planer, and a planed piece of pine (*Pinus* sp.) 5½ × 2⅜ × ⅜in (140 × 60 × 10mm) was sandwiched in between the two pieces of ash, with the grain running parallel to that of the ash.

Once the ash had been dimensioned and planed, a length of 240-grit abrasive was fixed to the table of my bandsaw with adhesive tape so the surfaces could be sanded smooth. All three pieces of wood were then sandwiched together using PVA glue. Newspaper was placed between each layer to enable them to be split apart once the project had been turned, with the pine section being removed and discarded. This allows you to create an oval box, which is more interesting than the standard cylindrical profile. You can modify or adapt the design as you see fit.

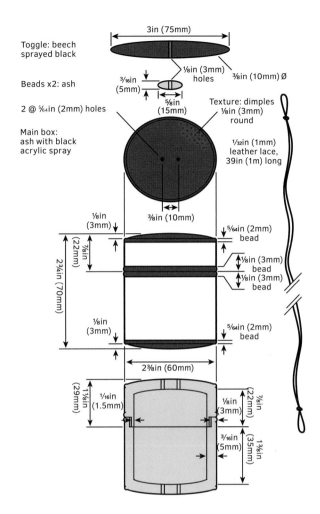

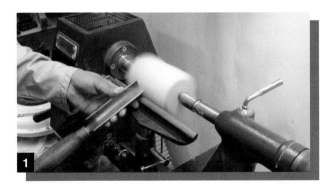

1 Accurately mark the centre of the blank, place between centres and rough down to the round using a spindle roughing gouge. Using callipers, check the diameter in several places along the blank. Use a ¼in (6mm) parting tool to clean up both faces of the blank. Produce a spigot at each end to suit your chuck jaws. Refine the spigot, with a skew held horizontally on the toolrest in trailing mode, to a dovetail profile, if your chuck requires it.

2 Using a ½in (12mm) skew chisel, refine the profile with planing cuts. Using a pencil, mark the sizes for the box and the lid section on the blank. The lid needs to be approximately one-third the length of the box body.

3 Using a ¼in (6mm) parting tool, part in centrally on the lid line to a depth of ³⁄₁₆in (5mm). Start with the parting tool laid horizontally on the toolrest – this will give a sharp edge and will prevent lifting the wood fibres at the edge. Using the toe of a ½in (12mm) skew chisel, define the beads at the top and base of the blank. Also, cut a slight angle at the top and bottom faces where the edges will meet, to give a sight line at the join.

4 Use a ⅛in (3mm) parting tool to part off the lid from the box. Leave ¹⁄₆₄in (0.5mm) of wood from the inside recess – this is used as a gauge or registration mark when opening out the inside of the box to obtain a good fit for the lid. In this instance I have left the spigot on the lid to fit inside the box, but if you prefer, a spigot can be left on the base section and the lid fitted onto this. Part through until ⅜in (10mm) of material is left, then remove the lid using a fine saw blade.

5 Tighten the lid of the box into the chuck jaws. Use a ¼in (6mm) spindle gouge, rotated anticlockwise and cutting on the left side of the tool at around 10 o'clock of the cutting edge. Hollow out the interior, leaving the profile of the lower part concave, as right-angled corners make it more difficult to remove small items from the box. Remove the waste, stopping short of the register material left when parting off.

6 The next step is to use a round-nose scraper to refine the inside profile of the box – I used a shearing cut.

7 Finish the interior using abrasive from 120 to 400 grit. Gently finish the exterior diameter of the spigot that will fit into the base. Be careful to keep this parallel or it may be difficult to achieve a good fit later. Use suitable lung protection at this stage.

8 Place the body of the box into the chuck and hollow out using a ¼in (6mm) spindle gouge, as before. Stop ¹⁄₃₂in (1mm) from the registration line. Using a ½in (12mm) skew chisel in a trailing mode, open out the interior diameter to achieve a tight fit with the lid. Continue to hollow out as before and finish with a round-nose scraper and abrasive. Only use fine abrasive within the recess area to achieve a good fit with the lid. Oversanding will loosen the fit too much.

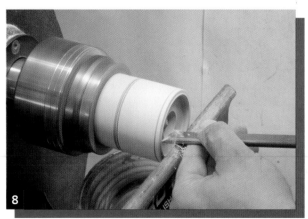

9 Turn a waste piece of sycamore (*Acer pseudoplatanus*) or other close-grained wood down to fit into the jaws of your chuck. Turn the profile down with a skew chisel until the lid of the box can be jammed onto the waste wood. I generally take the waste wood down until I have a tight fit with the box and refine with 320 abrasive until a good fit is achieved. However, due to the material being laminated in this case, achieve a light fit and bring up the tail centre for added support. Too tight a fit on the jam chuck could split the layers apart. Use a ¼in (6mm) spindle gouge to refine the top to a convex profile.

10 Using a point tool or skew in trailing mode, produce a groove near the outer edge of the lid. Finish with abrasive down to 400 grit. Now repeat the process for the body of the box.

11 Using a sharp knife, remove the waste wood on the ends of both the lid and the base. Finish with abrasive to blend in the profile. Place both parts onto a flat surface, and use a fine craft blade to carefully split down through the glue lines.

12 Place 320-grit abrasive on a flat surface and gently remove any residue of glue and paper. Be careful not to alter the flat surface of the face you are sanding.

13 Apply a fine layer of medium-viscosity cyanoacrylate and join the two halves of the box together. Hold them together with masking tape until fixed. Draw a centre line through on the top of both lid and base. Mark two points on this line centrally, ³⁄₁₆in (5mm) either side of the central point. Using a ⁵⁄₆₄in (2mm) drill – depending upon the thickness of the cord you are using – make two holes at these points through the lid and base.

14 Using a small round-nose engraving cutter in a rotary tool, produce a random texturing on the top of the lid and the underside of the box. Sand back the textured areas with 400-grit abrasive and treat the other parts with acrylic sanding sealer. Once dry, spray the inside.

15 Mask the main areas to be left natural; take care to slightly overlap the areas to be left into the grooves of the defining lines. Run your fingernail around the inside of each groove to fix the tape and prevent overspray onto these areas. Finish with several fine coats of acrylic black spray. Repeat for the inside of the box. Once dry, remove the masking tape and coat with acrylic satin lacquer.

16 Take a piece of waste beech (*Fagus sylvatica*) and cut down on the bandsaw to ⅝in (15mm) square by 4¼in (110mm) long. Mark halfway along the blank and drill a central ⅛in (3mm) hole. Place between centres and, using a ½in (12mm) skew chisel, produce the toggle profile so that the form is equal either side of the hole. Turn the ends down to a few millimetres. Finish the outside down to 400 grit by hand. Remove the toggle from the lathe and cut the waste material away using a sharp craft knife. Blend the ends with abrasive by hand down to 400 grit. Apply acrylic sanding sealer and allow to dry. Spray with acrylic black lacquer as before, allow to dry, and seal with acrylic satin lacquer.

17 Rough down a waste piece of ash to approximately ⅝in (15mm) to fit into the jaws of the chuck. Here I am using button jaws. Clean up the front face using the toe of a ½in (12mm) skew chisel. Using a Jacobs chuck, drill a ⅛in (3mm) hole through the centre of the blank, deep enough so that you can produce two beads around ¼in (6mm) thick.

18 Using the ½in (12mm) skew chisel, round over the front face of the bead. Finish with 400-grit abrasive and use the toe of the skew to produce the back profile of the bead to replicate the front. Once achieved, the bead can be sliced off with the skew. Finish the back of the bead by hand, if required, down to 400 grit. Repeat for the second bead, then coat with acrylic sanding sealer and acrylic satin lacquer.

19 Fold the cord in half and tie a knot near the folded end. Feed the cord ends through the first bead and up through the two holes in the base of the box. Feed the ends through the top of the box from the inside; make sure the grain of both parts is aligned before doing this. Feed through the next bead and the toggle, then tie the cord to join the ends. Your box is now complete.

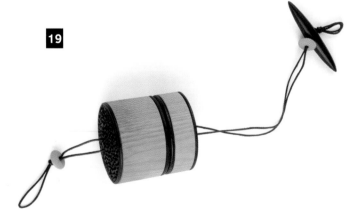

BOX WITH CARVED HANDLE

A handle formed in one piece with the lid is the distinctive
feature of this gracefully proportioned box by Neil Scobie.
It is not a particularly difficult project to make, but does offer
a few challenges in both the turning and the carving.

WHAT YOU NEED

- Australian red cedar, approx. 7in (180mm) diameter
  × 3in (75mm) deep
- Small deep-fluted gouge
- Small spindle gouge
- Parting tool
- Round skew chisel
- Bandsaw
- Fine-blade saw
- Carving burrs
- Dividers
- Various grits of abrasives

- 0000 steel wool
- Masking tape
- Soft pencil – 4B or 6B
- ⁵⁄₁₆in (8mm) no. 7 carving gouge
- Rotary carving tool, ¼in (6mm) diameter with
  rounded end and straight shank
- Disc sander
- Oil sealer
- PPE: face mask, respirator/dust mask
  and extraction

INTRODUCTION

I almost always turn lidded boxes on
end grain so I do not have to worry
about movement in the fit of the lid.
However, for this project, an endgrain
orientation will not really work with
the handle, so my choice is to use a
sidegrain blank of quartersawn timber.
Quartersawing means that the grain
will run vertically in the turned box
when you look from the end grain.
In the turning process, you may
encounter some movement in the
timber due to stresses built up in
the blank. If it does move, you may
need to re-turn either the box section
or the lid. The timber I have chosen
is Australian red cedar (*Toona ciliata*),
but you could use any timber of
your choosing.

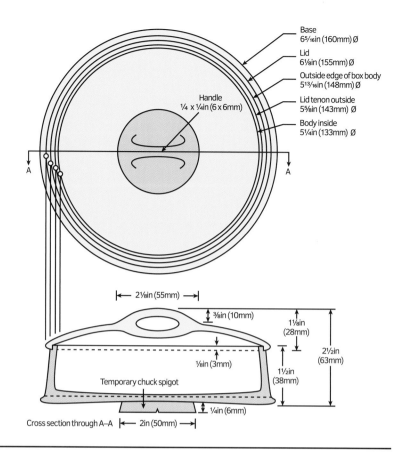

Base
6⁵⁄₁₆in (160mm) Ø

Lid
6¹⁄₈in (155mm) Ø

Outside edge of box body
5¹³⁄₁₆in (148mm) Ø

Lid tenon outside
5⅝in (143mm) Ø

Body inside
5¼in (133mm) Ø

Handle
¼ x ¼in (6 x 6mm)

2⅛in (55mm)

⅜in (10mm)

1⅛in (28mm)

2½in (63mm)

⅛in (3mm)

1½in (38mm)

Temporary chuck spigot

¼in (6mm)

Cross section through A–A 2in (50mm)

1 Bandsaw the blank, then open the jaws of
your scroll chuck a little before placing the
blank against the jaws with the tailstock centre
pressing in the centre. Alternatively, place the
blank between centres to turn a chucking spigot.
A screw centre is not an option here, as you don't
want a screw hole in either the top or base of the
blank. Use a small bowl gouge to trim the waste
off and turn on centre.

2 Turning from the outside towards the centre
to avoid chip-out at the edges, trim up the
base and make a spigot to suit your scroll chuck.
This will be the base side of the box.

3 Use a round skew chisel to turn a slight
dovetail shape on the spigot to suit the jaws
of the scroll chuck. This temporary spigot will be
turned off at the very end.

4 Turn the blank around and hold the base spigot in the scroll chuck. Now you can remove the tailstock and turn a spigot on the top side of the blank. This spigot will later be reshaped into the handle. Cut from the centre towards the rim – you will be cutting with the grain because of the slope of the domed lid.

5 Here you can see the finished shape of the top of the lid, with the scroll chuck spigot where the handle will be.

6 The next step is to turn the side profile of the box, using either a spindle gouge or a small bowl gouge. Turn from around the middle section towards the top and bottom beads. The beads should protrude around ⅛in or so (3–4mm) above the side wall.

7 To get the definition between the side wall and the beads, you will need to roll a spindle gouge over on its side so you can cut right into the corner of the bead. You can cut both ways into the corner. This process should be carried out on the lid bead and the bottom bead.

8 To part off the lid of the box, you should take two cuts to give the tool side clearance. For this deep parting cut you will need to hold the parting tool securely and stop when you have about ⅝in (15mm) left to saw off by hand.

9 Place the lid spigot in a scroll chuck and use dividers to mark the diameter of the step on the inside of the lid; check the drawing for sizes. If you are using the dividers with the lathe spinning, make sure you engage the left-hand side of the dividers first, so it is supported by the toolrest.

10 Use a skew chisel to cut the step in the inside of the lid. This should be about ⁵⁄₆₄–⅛in (2–3mm) deep and parallel to the axis of the lid.

11 Use a small bowl gouge to shape the inside dome to allow for the undercutting of the handle on the top of the lid. Depending on how deep you want to make the handle, allow enough depth in the dome to leave about ⁵⁄₃₂in (4mm) thickness after the handle carving is finished.

12 You can now completely sand the underside of the lid up to 400 grit, making sure all marks have been removed.

13 Here you can see the completed underside of the lid.

14 Now place the base spigot in the scroll chuck and turn out the inside part of the box. This is the same process as turning the inside of a bowl. Cut from the rim towards the middle in order to cut with the grain. You should be looking for a base thickness of about 3/16–1/4in (5–6mm) to allow for the slight undercut of the base. The wall thickness should be the same. You can have a rounded or a square internal corner, depending on your preference.

15 Once the inside is finished, take trim cuts off the outside in case the blank has warped out of round in the process of hollowing the inside. You may also need to trim the tenon so the lid is a tight fit. Fully sand the base section with 180 grit to start, working up to 400 grit, followed by 0000 steel wool to polish the surface of the box.

16 Push the lid onto the tenon of the base ready to turn the handle section. If the lid is a little loose, just wrap the join with a couple of runs of masking tape. You should now be able to trim the top surface of the lid and the raised section of the handle. Leave a small section around the tailstock centre. You can then fully sand the top of the lid up to the small tailstock spigot; it is best to do this while the lid is spinning.

17 While the box is spinning, use a soft pencil, such as a 4B or 6B, to mark a circle where the lid hollow is contained.

18 After removing the small spigot that you left in step 16, draw in the handle carving area. Refer back to the drawing for the measurements.

19 The carving can be done with hand carving tools quite successfully, as long as you are carving with the grain. Basically, you need to carve down the hill towards the lowest point from all sides. A small gouge such as a 5/16in (8mm) number 7 will do the job.

20 I think it is much easier to use rotary tools for the handle carving, as you do not need to worry about grain direction and it is much quicker. You can choose from any number of rotary tools to drive burrs for carving, including high-speed versions. The burr best suited would be one about ¼in (6mm) in diameter with a rounded end and a straight shank. You can use the burr while the box is held in a vice so you can support the handpiece in both hands.

21 Make yourself comfortable sitting down and support your hand on your leg while carving out under the handle; this position allows you to keep rotating the box as you work around the handle.

22 To sand the carved area, a small disc sander is the best way to go. I am using a dedicated handpiece that hooks onto a rotary carving unit. The abrasive is held onto the small soft leather disc by double-sided tape. This is cheap to buy and quick to change to the next grit. Look for the sponge or foam double-sided tape, which is about ⅛in (3mm) thick.

23 To sand under the handle of the box, hold the chuck in a vice and hold the bottom spigot in the chuck so you have both hands free to pull a thin strip of cloth-backed abrasive backwards and forwards. Work down to 400 grit until all the scratches have been removed. Note that the lid has been taped on so it will not come off while sanding. Hand-sand with the grain to remove any scratches left by the rotary sander. Sand to 400 grit, followed by 0000 steel wool. Check the fit of your lid; if it is too tight, place it back on the lathe and take a trim cut off the tenon – or maybe a quick sand with a piece of 320-grit abrasive will do.

24 Make a jam-fit chuck to place the bottom half of the box onto so that you can turn off the bottom spigot. Use a small deep-fluted gouge, cutting towards the centre. The base should have a slight hollow towards the centre.

25 Sand the base completely, and the box should now be ready for finishing. I used four coats of oil sealer on this box, with a light sand with 0000 steel wool between coats.

RABBIT BOX

Bob Chapman created this playful design by cutting and recombining the sections of what is basically a winged bowl. The result is both striking and fun.

INTRODUCTION

To introduce an element of experimentation and uncertainty into my work, I am becoming more and more interested in cutting up the initial shapes that I produce and then rejoining the pieces in an attempt to discover structural forms which appeal to me.

When I see a new shape, the problem is, 'How do I recreate that shape?' and with a new technique the question is, 'What shapes might this lead to?' I had thought about what might be obtained by cutting a winged bowl lengthways, and had made some simple models to help visualize the result. I decided that a bowl with curved wings would make an interesting design, which would be quite stable standing on end without support.

The wings curving upwards suggested a rabbit's ears, and from there it was a short step to the concept of a 'rabbit'. The idea of making the rabbit into a box arose from the need for a face to complete the rabbit image.

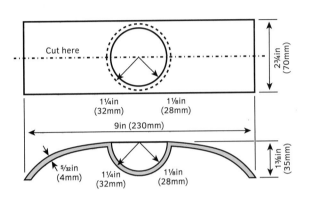
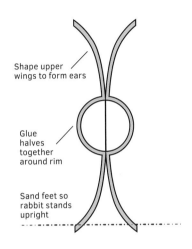

1 You will need a piece of European sycamore (*Acer pseudoplatanus*), 11¾ × 2¾ × 1⅜in (300 × 70 × 35mm). Cut a short section 2¾in (70mm) long from one end and retain this for the face of the rabbit. Mount the remaining 9in (230mm) piece centrally on a ⁵⁄₁₆in (8mm) screw held in the scroll chuck. Gradually increase the speed to around 2,000rpm.

2 Use a ½in (12mm) bowl gouge to shape the concave side of the wings and roughly shape the outside of the bowl part. Make sure a smooth curve is achieved here, as you will not be able to refine this shape later except by hand-sanding with the lathe switched off.

3 Form a shallow spigot with the corner of a skew chisel to allow the piece to be reversed in the chuck. Note the black line on the toolrest to remind me where the ends of the wings are as they rotate.

4 With the piece held on the spigot, shape the convex side of the wings with the bowl gouge. As the blank rotates the thickness of the wings can clearly be seen, and this allows an even thickness of around $\frac{5}{32}$–$\frac{3}{16}$in (4–5mm) to be obtained. Keep the toolrest close to the work and take light cuts.

5 Use a ½in (12mm) bowl gouge to hollow the bowl section, then refine with a 1in (25mm) round-nose scraper. The bowl is well supported by the chuck jaws and this operation is quite straightforward, but don't forget the wings are still there!

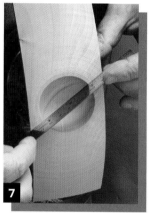

6 It's important that the cross section of the bowl is semicircular, and a cardboard template is a great help in ensuring this.

7 The rim of the bowl must be flat, since later it will be folded over and glued to itself. The mating surfaces are only about $\frac{5}{32}$in (4mm) wide and must meet properly if the glue joint is to be secure.

8 Form a jam chuck from scrap wood, which needs to be shaped to fit the bowl's interior.

9 With the workpiece securely held in the jam chuck, the outside of the bowl can be shaped. Use another template to ensure an even wall thickness of approximately $\frac{5}{32}$in (4mm).

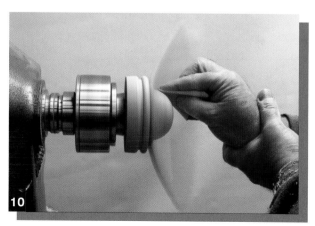

10 The outside of the bowl can be sanded with the lathe running, but don't attempt to sand the wings this way – stop the lathe and hand-sand these from 120 down to 400 grit. Sycamore is a pale timber already, but I particularly wanted to make a white rabbit. Give the bowl three applications of wood bleach, taking care to follow the instructions on the box. Not only will this bleach the wood to a pale creamy white, it will also raise the grain, and when sanded down again with 400 grit, a silky-smooth finish is obtained.

11 After carefully marking the midpoint, cut the bowl in half lengthways on the bandsaw. The saw is also used for the initial shaping of the ears. Note how you can cut off one of the ears and re-attach at an angle to give it the impression of flopping forwards a little.

12 Use a sanding disc on the lathe to refine the shape of the ears, rounding the edges and thinning the ears slightly towards the tips.

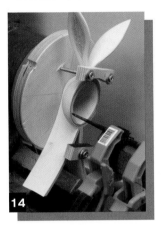

13 Using a rotary tool with a small ball-shaped burr attachment, texture what will be the inner surface of the rabbit's ear. This cuts through the bleached surface, and the creamy-brown wood underneath gives a pleasing contrast to the ear.

14 Turning a shoulder on what will become the body of the box is problematic. My solution was to clamp the rabbit to a plywood base which was held on the vacuum chuck. Partially releasing the vacuum allowed the whole assembly to slide around on the face of the chuck until the correct position was found. The vacuum was then increased to grip the base plate in that position. A metal scriber clamped to the toolrest was used to indicate the best position.

15 Use a ⅛in (3mm) parting tool to cut a small shoulder on the front of the box section to take the lid of the box, which will form the rabbit's face.

16 With the shoulder cut, sand the rabbit's feet level on the sanding disc so that the box will now stand upright. Bleach the interior of the box again where the surface has been removed.

17 Hold a small screw chuck in the scroll chuck and mount the 2¾in (70mm) square section which was set aside in step 1. This small block will become the face of the rabbit and the lid of the box. After roughing the block to a dome shape, cut a small dovetail spigot in the front, using the long point of a skew as a scraper.

18 Reverse the block with the dovetail spigot held in the chuck jaws and form a parallel-sided spigot to be a good fit inside the rabbit box.

19 The lid must fit well because the box will be on its side and a loose-fitting lid would fall off. On the other hand, a too tightly fitting lid is difficult to remove. At this point I accidentally broke off the floppy ear and decided to leave it off until I got the fit of the face right.

20 Once the fit is right, hollow out the face to about ¼in (6mm) thick.

21 Reverse the face into a small jam chuck made from scrap wood and shape the front surface to a rounded dome. With the lathe stopped, drill two shallow ⁵⁄₁₆in (8mm) holes with a Forstner bit to take the rabbit's eyes.

22 The eyes are made from ebony (*Diospyros* sp.) dowel, turned to a good fit in the holes. Glue short sections into the holes, return the face to the jam chuck and skim the eyes flush with the face. Next, a small drum sander in the rotary tool helps shape the face. Rabbits have narrow faces, and the round shape obtained by turning needs modifying as much as the overall shape and thickness of the wood will allow. Use the sander to give the face a slightly flattened forehead and the suggestion of a nose. Where the face overlaps the sides slightly, use the sander to blend the two. Then bleach the face to match the rest of the piece. Hand-sand the whole rabbit to 400 grit and seal with cellulose sanding sealer. Rub down with steel wool and apply a thin coat of lemon oil, rubbing in with a cloth before allowing to dry.

23 Sketch the bow tie on a piece of card and adjust for size before cutting out of a piece of ebony, which needs to measure about ⁵⁄₁₆in (8mm) thick. Sand the bow tie and shape with the rotary tool before sealing and polishing on a buffing wheel. Glue in place with a drop of cyanoacrylate.

HANDY HINTS

- When mounting the blank, centre it accurately so it is balanced when it starts to rotate. Start the lathe at a slow speed and increase gradually. The faster the piece is rotating, the quicker the corners come round and the more 'solid' it will seem. Note where the ends of the blank are, and keep your fingers out of the way. Wear full-face protection.

- Although the workpiece was a good fit on the jam chuck, I was worried that any movement would wreck the wings if they hit the toolrest. To prevent this I used two or three small dabs of hot-melt glue to secure it in place. This worked very well and I later found it surprisingly difficult to separate the two pieces, despite using a hot-air gun to melt the glue.

- The curvature of the wings makes getting the ½in (12mm) bowl gouge into the corner between the wings and the bowl rather difficult. A shallow-fluted spindle gouge with a long grind makes it a lot easier.

ORIENTAL-STYLE BOX

This sycamore box by Mark Sanger features a scorched and deeply textured surface, and a handle derived from the *Torii* or entrance gates of Japanese temples. You can also make a plinth to show it off.

WHAT YOU NEED

- Endgrain sycamore blank, 100 x 100 x 130m (4 × 4 × 5⅛in)
- Prepared sycamore offcut, 90 × 35 × 10 (3½ × 1⅜ × ⅜in)
- Prepared sycamore offcut, 60 × 60 x 30mm (2⅜ × 2⅜ × 1⅛in) for the plinth
- 1in (25mm) spindle roughing gouge
- ⅜in (10mm) spindle gouge
- ½in (12mm) skew chisel
- ⅛in (3mm) parting tool
- Skew chisel
- ¼in (6mm) parting tool
- ¼in (6mm) point tool
- Abrasives, 120–320 grit
- Fine-blade saw
- 1in (25mm) round-nose scraper
- ³⁄₆₄in (1mm) ball-nose cutter in a rotary tool
- Scrollsaw or coping saw
- Chisel or power carver
- Butane-propane-mix blowtorch
- Acrylic spray sanding sealer
- 0000 wire wool
- Antique mahogany spirit stain
- Medium-viscosity cyanoacrylate (superglue)
- Small foam surface protection pads (optional)

INTRODUCTION

This simple box uses a blank of endgrain sycamore (*Acer pseudoplatanus*) 100mm (4in) square. It also uses one of the simplest ways of producing a box, which is to part the top from the main form and re-insert this back into a recess.

Both the main form and handle are scorched to provide a contrast to the lid and the plinth on which the finished box sits. However, the scorching could just as easily be replaced by acrylic spray paint to add a touch of colour. If you prefer the box without the texturing and scorching, just miss these steps out and finish with abrasive before applying your preferred finish. Beads can also be used to replace the texturing for a different effect, and the form of the box can be altered to suit your own personal tastes.

The box is hollowed using a standard spindle gouge, so there is no need for specialist tools here. However, if you choose to make the box deeper in profile, then you can use a small hollowing tool to achieve this.

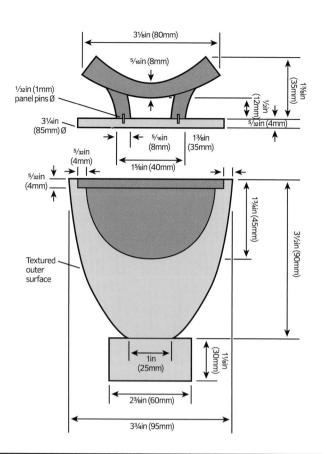

1 Accurately mark the centres at each end of the blank, place between centres and rough down to the round with a 1in (25mm) spindle roughing gouge.

2 Using a ¼in (6mm) parting tool, clean up both ends of the blank by parting in at a safe distance from the drive and tail centres.

3 Produce a spigot at one end using the ¼in (6mm) parting tool and refine with a ½in (12mm) skew chisel held horizontal on the toolrest to produce the correct profile to fit your chuck jaws.

4 Reverse the blank into the chuck and tighten. Using a ½in (12mm) skew chisel, clean up the front face, making sure the face is flat by checking with a straightedge with the lathe stationary.

5 Using a ¼in (6mm) parting tool, part in at the end nearest to the tail centre to a depth of approximately ³⁄₁₆in (5mm). Move the tool to the left and take a second cut to the same depth, so that a spigot is produced that is about ½in (12mm) wide. Make sure that the spigot is parallel, as it will need to be fitted into a recess at a later stage; if tapered, it will leave an unsightly gap at the join.

6 Finish the top face and outer edge with abrasive from 120 to 320 grit. Gently blend the sharp outer edge of the top to a small radius. This will soften the join when reinserted.

7 Using a ³⁄₈in (10mm) spindle gouge, rough down the outside to start producing the desired profile. Leave the form thicker towards the base, as you want to retain rigidity for the hollowing process; the shape will be refined later. Using a ⅛in (3mm) parting tool, part slightly to the right of the shoulder of the main form where it meets the lid; this will leave a small amount of material for registration when you come to size the recess for the lid at a later stage. If required, widen the cut slightly as you progress; this will prevent the tool from binding.

8 With the lathe stationary, cut the remaining waste away using a fine saw blade. Or, if you are confident, the top can be parted off in one go by holding the thin parting tool in one hand and gently holding the lid with the other.

9 Using a ³⁄₈in (10mm) spindle gouge, open out the inside from the centre to approximately ³⁄₈in (10mm) deep and ¼in (6mm) short of the registration mark formed in step 7.

10 Using a ¼in (6mm) parting tool, produce a recess in the front face ⁵⁄₆₄–⅛in (2–3mm) less in depth than the thickness of the lid. Angle the tool in slightly to start with, to produce a slight taper. Offer up the lid and once it starts to fit, make the recess parallel by taking fine cuts until it fits down inside the top with a small amount protruding.

11 Stick masking tape across the top of the lid with extra protruding each side, insert the lid with the unfinished side facing out and push down into the recess to lightly jam it in. Fold the excess masking tape over and stick to the outside of the form. Using a ³⁄₈in (10mm) spindle gouge, finish the underside of the lid.

12 Using a ¼in (6mm) point tool, produce several grooves in the base for interest and finish by hand with abrasive down to 320 grit. Once complete, use the masking tape previously left protruding to remove the lid by pulling both ends of the tape gently out, thus removing the lid from the form.

13 Continue using the ⅜in (10mm) spindle gouge to open out the remaining internal profile, leaving the wall ⅜–⁹⁄₁₆in (10–15mm) thick and the shoulder approximately ⁵⁄₁₆in (8mm) wide for the lid to sit on. Blend the profile thicker as you progress towards the base. Rotate the tool anticlockwise and cut left of the tip to do this – or you could use a small hollowing tool. Refine the surface with a 1in (25mm) round-nose scraper. Finish the inside by power-sanding with abrasive from 120 to 320 grit. Finish the recess and shoulder down to 320 grit by hand, taking care not to remove too much material. Blend over the outer sharp corner of the recess that will sit next to the lid.

14 Using a ⅜in (10mm) spindle gouge, refine the outside profile towards the base, working from the outside diameter in. Turn in so that there is approximately ⁹⁄₁₆in (15mm) of waste remaining.

15 Produce a friction-drive chuck to fit inside the form and reverse between centres, using kitchen towel between the chuck and the form to prevent marking. Remove the remaining waste and blend into the base using a ⅜in (10mm) spindle gouge, leaving approximately ³⁄₁₆in (5mm) of the spigot remaining. Refine the base area with a ½in (12mm) skew chisel and cut in with the toe to concave the base. Alternatively, use a parting tool or a ¼in (6mm) spindle gouge.

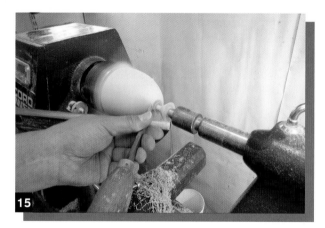

16 Cut through the remaining waste with a fine saw blade, blending the last bit using a sharp chisel or a power carver. Finally finish by hand down to 320 grit. Using a ³⁄₆₄in (1mm) ball-nose cutter in a rotary tool, produce the outside texture to a depth of around ³⁄₆₄–⁵⁄₆₄in (1–2mm), blending this up onto the rim at the top.

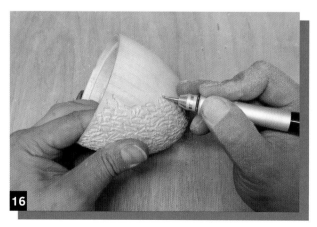

17 Before scorching, vacuum up all the shavings or dust and make sure a fire extinguisher is close to hand – or work outside. Gently rub over the surface with 240 grit and scorch the outside and rim using a butane–propane-mix blowtorch. Keep moving the flame over the surface. Allow to cool and repeat until the surface is heavily scorched.

18 Allow to fully cool and apply a coat of antique mahogany spirit stain.

19 Spray the outside and inside with several fine coats of acrylic sanding sealer. If required, cut back the inside by hand with 0000 wire wool. You can apply a top coat of satin lacquer if you choose to.

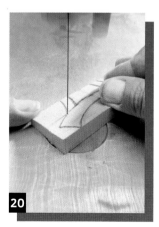 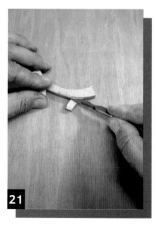

20 Take a piece of sycamore measuring 90 × 35 × 10 (3½ × 1⅜ × ⅜in). Finish the faces by hand down to 240 grit. Draw the design onto the surface using a pencil and cut this out on a scrollsaw or by hand with a coping saw.

21 Incise the radius of the top horizontal section joining the uprights, using a sharp craft knife on both sides. You can then reduce the thickness of the uprights equally on each side until both are approximately ³⁄₁₆in (5mm) thick.

22 Refine and finish the faces and edges using abrasive from 120 to 240 grit stuck to thin pieces of wood.

23 Mark the centre and drill a ³⁄₆₄in (1mm) diameter hole in each upright to a depth of approximately ⁵⁄₆₄in (2mm).

24 Take two panel pins and cut them both to a length of ⁵⁄₃₂–³⁄₁₆in (4–5mm) using wire cutters. Drip medium-viscosity cyanoacrylate into the hole, push in the cut ends of the pins and allow to dry. Mark a centre line on the lid of the box using a pencil and rule. Hold the handle in position, centralize by eye and push the pins into the surface to leave a mark, using the pencil line as a gauge. Use the ³⁄₆₄in (1mm) drill to bore the holes to a depth of ⁵⁄₆₄–¹⁄₈in (2–3mm), being careful not to drill through the lid.

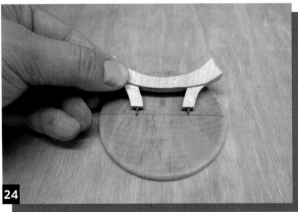

25 Place the handle on a non-flammable surface and scorch using a blowtorch as before. Keep scorching until small surface cracks appear in the wood, this being an interesting texture to complement the body of the box. You will need to scorch the wood quite hard to achieve this effect. Expect the edges to glow and to round over or soften. Keep a damp cloth close to hand and dampen any edges that continue to glow after the flame is moved away from the handle.

26 Allow the project to fully cool, then spray with several coats of acrylic sanding sealer; this will seal the carbon onto the surface of the form. Allow to dry, then drip a small amount of medium-viscosity cyanoacrylate into the holes in the lid, push the handle with its panel pins in place and apply light pressure until the glue is set. Allow to harden and apply several fine coats of acrylic sanding sealer to the lid and handle, followed by a fine coat of acrylic satin lacquer.

27 Prepare a plinth for the box measuring 60 × 60 × 30mm (2³⁄₈ × 2³⁄₈ × 1¹⁄₈in), finish to 320-grit abrasive, spray with acrylic sanding sealer and apply several fine coats of acrylic satin lacquer to the surface. Then apply three small surface protector pads to the underside of the plinth; this will prevent it from scratching any highly polished surfaces it may be placed on. The final step is to insert the lid into the box and place the box on the plinth. The Oriental box project is now complete.

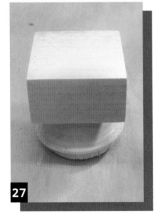

SEEDPOD-INSPIRED DECORATIVE BOX

Nick Arnull takes inspiration from nature to create and texture this beautiful box, which is made from a piece of English sycamore.

INTRODUCTION

For some time I have had a fascination with seedpods and poppy heads. Images of them found on the Internet inspired this design. The key element for a seedpod is usually the large body, which can often be quite bland but heavily shaped, in comparison to the much smaller top or stalk which is usually considerably more decorative and interesting.

I have tried to convey the colours of autumn within this piece, using an airbrush to apply artists'-quality inks. The texture and decoration are created using a high-powered pyrography machine. The carving on the body is completed using a rotary handpiece fitted with a carving burr. This project is made using English sycamore (*Acer pseudoplatanus*).

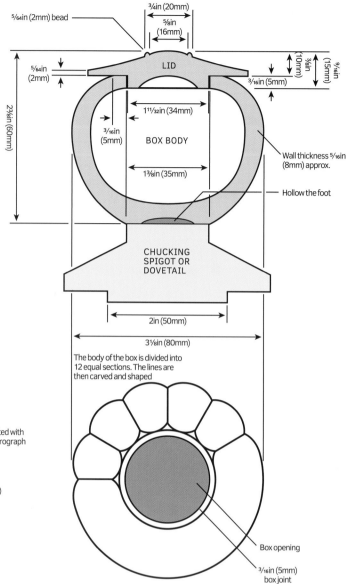

¾in (20mm)
⁵⁄₆₄in (2mm) bead
⅝in (16mm)
LID
⁵⁄₆₄in (2mm)
⅜in (10mm)
¾in (15mm)
⁹⁄₁₆in
³⁄₁₆in (5mm)
2⅜in (60mm)
1¹¹⁄₃₂in (34mm)
³⁄₁₆in (5mm)
BOX BODY
Wall thickness ⁵⁄₁₆in (8mm) approx.
1⅜in (35mm)
Hollow the foot
CHUCKING SPIGOT OR DOVETAIL
2in (50mm)
3⅛in (80mm)

The body of the box is divided into 12 equal sections. The lines are then carved and shaped

Box opening
³⁄₁₆in (5mm) box joint

Dotted lines help when marking out the design. The lid is divided equally by 12

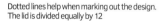

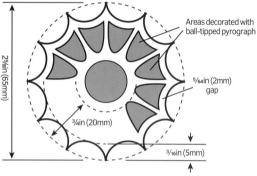

Areas decorated with ball-tipped pyrograph
⁵⁄₆₄in (2mm) gap
2⅝in (65mm)
¾in (20mm)
³⁄₁₆in (5mm)

1 First select your timber, mount it between centres and make round using a 1¼in (32mm) spindle roughing gouge. Then create a spigot at one end of the timber to fit into your chuck.

2 Mark the length of the box and begin to shape the body using a ⅜in (10mm) spindle gouge.

3 Begin to refine the outside shape using a freshly sharpened spindle gouge.

4 Define the final length of the body using a ¼in (6mm) parting tool.

5 Remove some of the waste timber towards the chuck; this will give access when carving the body later on.

6 Finally, shear-scrape the outside of the box with a ⅜in (10mm) round skew chisel.

7 Mark the diameter of the opening at 1⅜in (35mm) and create a ³⁄₁₆in (5mm) flat at the top of the box; this will later become part of the box-lid joint.

8 Begin to hollow out the inside of the box using a ⅜in (10mm) spindle gouge. Take care to avoid damaging the opening; this will need to be tooled accurately using a square-end box scraper.

9 Refine the interior of the box with a small multi-tipped scraper.

10 Sand the inside and outside of the box at this stage. Apply sanding sealer to the inside only and de-nib.

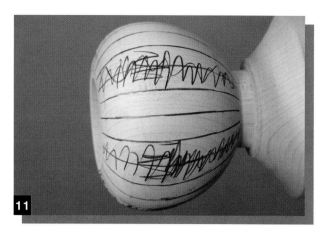

11 Divide the outside of the piece equally into 24 sections. Each of the fluted segments of the body occupies two of these 24 sections. (The remaining lines indicate the centre line of each segment, providing a useful reference when carving.)

12 Carve down the boundary lines using a V-gouge to produce the grooves between the segments.

13 Next, begin to soften the edges using a carving burr fitted into a rotary handpiece.

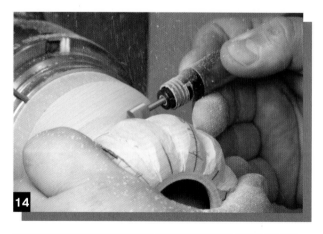

14 Remove the waste timber on the opposite side of each segment to complete the rough shaping of the body. Try to maintain the position and direction of the carved line as work progresses.

15 Begin to sand the carved areas; I use an old toothbrush that has been modified to accept hook-and-loop abrasives – this really does speed things along. Final sanding is best done by hand, taking your time to achieve the best results possible. As you work through the various grades, use water to raise the grain, allow to dry, then re-sand. Once you are happy with the sanding, seal the outside of the box using acrylic spray sanding sealer.

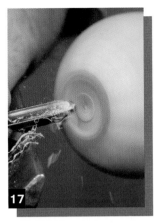

16 With the carving and sanding complete, reduce the spigot at the base of the box. Then, with the lathe stationary, cut it free with a fine-tooth saw.

17 Using the scrap wood left in the chuck, create a tight-fitting jam chuck and fit the box onto this, then carefully remove the waste timber and refine the base of the box. Sand and seal.

18 Begin by mounting the blank between centres, then create a spigot to hold the blank into the chuck.

19 Mount the blank into the chuck and create the spigot to fit into the box opening. Dish the centre; this area will become the underside of the box lid.

20 Reduce the lid to a diameter of 2⅝in (65mm).

21 Sand the lid rim and the centre of the lid.

22 Create a tight-fitting jam chuck and drill a hole through the centre of it. Reverse-chuck the lid and turn the outer top profile. You can sand at this stage.

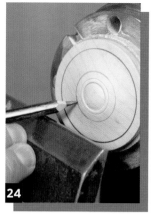

23 Mark and turn a small bead at the centre of the lid, then create a cushioned button at the very centre.

24 Using a small drum sander, shape the edge of the lid, working towards the line previously marked; take care at this stage to ensure a balanced design as in the drawing. Mark two lines at ³⁄₁₆in (5mm) and ³⁄₄in (20mm) in from the outside edge. Using your lathe's indexing head, mark the 12 points around the outer edge of the lid.

25 Mark the design onto the lid top and begin to burn it in using a pyrograph; these lines will become the boundaries of the textured areas.

26 Using a small ball-tip in the pyrograph, create the dimples in the surface of the top. The temperature will need to be quite high to achieve this. Use a soft bronze brush to remove any carbon, when the burning is complete and before beginning to apply colour.

27 Using a fish-scale tip fitted into the handpiece, create the outer border of the design around the inside of the lid. Add a second row to provide a visual boundary to the design. Then add a bead at the centre to give the design visual balance. Add texture to the area using the ball-tipped handpiece as before.

28 With the body jammed onto a tapered stick, apply a base colour of raw sienna using an artist's airbrush. It may take several layers to achieve an even coverage.

29 Add shading and variation using Vandyke brown. This will add depth to the design. When you are happy with the colouring, leave it to dry. Seal the surface using an acrylic satin lacquer – multiple light coats are best here.

30 Repeat the same steps to colour the lid. Placing the lid back into its jam chuck will make it easier to handle while painting. Allow to dry before sealing with acrylic satin lacquer. The seedpod box is now complete.

HANDY HINTS

- Moisten the timber to raise the grain when sanding; this will help you to achieve a better overall finish.

- Define textured areas with a clear boundary.

- Always sharpen your tools before making a finishing cut.

- Keep your colour palette to a minimum.

- Seal the surface before spraying with acrylic colours.

- Make use of jam chucks where possible. Anticipate how the workpiece might be removed from the jam chuck after being worked. For example, a simple hole through the centre of the chuck would allow a rod to be inserted to push it out. Applying water to jam chucks will ensure that they hold a little tighter.

- Try to finish every part of a decorated box to an equal standard.

- Try working at a smaller scale when producing decorative items.

GLOSSARY

bead a convex half-round profile.

between centres (of a workpiece) mounted in the lathe so that one end is pressed against the drive centre in the headstock, and the other against the live or dead centre in the tailstock, without any need for a chuck.

blank a piece of material which has been reduced to a convenient size and shape in preparation for further work to be carried out on it.

CAD computer-assisted drawing: a generic name given to various computer programs used in design work.

chatter vibration of a tool during cutting, leaving a series of ripple-like marks in the wood; this is usually undesirable, but may sometimes be used as a decorative feature.

cove a concave quarter-round profile.

de-nib to abrade a finished surface lightly so as to remove small bumps and protrusions ('nibs') without removing all the finish.

downhill following the grain of the wood so that the fibres cannot be caught or torn by the cutting edge.

end grain the transverse surface of wood, revealed by cutting across the fibres.

fingernail grind a way of shaping a woodturning gouge so that the centre of the cutting edge projects forward and the corners slope back.

flute the concave (hollow) side of a gouge.

friction chuck *see* jam chuck.

granny-tooth scraper a scraper which has been ground down at the sides to leave only a narrow cutting edge in the middle, resembling a single tooth.

green wood wood that has not been dried or seasoned before use; it is very likely to distort after working, and this may be exploited as a decorative feature.

hardwood wood from a broadleaved tree, which tends to be harder than that from a conifer.

heartwood the harder wood produced near the centre of the tree trunk, as opposed to sapwood, formed in the outer layers of the tree. In some species, sapwood and heartwood differ greatly in colour.

heat-checking the formation of small cracks (checks) in wood when it is overheated, e.g. by excessively vigorous use of abrasives.

inclusions any extraneous matter, such as fragments of bark, that may be found embedded in a piece of wood.

jam chuck (or jam-fit chuck; also friction chuck) a temporary chuck made by mounting a piece of scrap wood in the lathe chuck and forming a hole or spigot in it, into or onto which the workpiece can be tightly fitted (jammed).

natural edge the unworked outer surface of a log or branch, often including the bark, retained in the finished work as a decorative feature.

pith the central part of a trunk or branch, usually avoided in woodwork because its presence may cause the wood to distort.

PPE personal protection equipment, such as face masks and respirators.

quartersawn sawn so that the growth rings in the timber are perpendicular to the surface; this minimizes subsequent warping or distortion of the wood.

sacrificial board an expendable piece of wood which is used to prevent damage to the workpiece, e.g. by placing it underneath a piece to be drilled so that any splintering which occurs damages only the sacrificial piece.

safety cloth a polishing cloth which is designed to tear easily if it becomes entangled in the lathe, so as not to pull the user's fingers into the work.

sanding through the grits (or grades) sanding using progressively finer grades of abrasive, so that each grade removes the scratches made by the previous one.

sapwood the softer wood formed in the outer layers of the growing tree, as opposed to heartwood from nearer the centre of the trunk. In some species, sapwood and heartwood differ greatly in colour.

shake a split in wood, caused by trauma, internal stresses or unequal moisture loss.

shear-scraping using a scraper with its cutting edge at around 45° to the lathe rotation; this allows very fine finishing cuts to be made, even against the grain.

softwood wood from a conifer, which tends to be softer than that from a broadleaved tree.

sp. (plural: spp.) abbreviation for 'species'.

spalting a pattern of irregular dark and light patches, often outlined with narrow black lines, caused by a fungal infection in the growing tree. It is usually regarded as a decorative feature, though it may weaken the wood to some extent.

spindle grain the orientation of the workpiece so that the grain runs parallel to the lathe axis, as in between centres turning.

tearout breaking or tearing of the wood fibres, caused e.g. by cutting against the grain.

trailing mode the method of presenting a tool to the work so that the handle is a little higher than the cutting edge, to reduce the risk of digging in.

CONTRIBUTORS

GMC Publications would like to thank the following contributors for their inspirational projects:

Nick Arnull Kitchen storage jars, Trio of nesting boxes, Seedpod-inspired decorative box; **Mark Baker** Box collection; **Bob Chapman** Three yew boxes, Spinning top box, Rabbit box; **Sue Harker** Snowman money box; **Dennis Keeling** Tunbridge ware box; **Mike Mahoney** Sugar bowl; **Tracy Owen** Lidded box; **Andrew Potocnik** Recycled yarran form, Jarrah burr box, Hybrid box; **Mark Sanger** Endgrain boxes, Crossgrain box, Curved box, Offset lidded form, Lidded form with finial, Japanese-inspired jewellery box, Japanese-style inro box, Oriental-style box; **Neil Scobie** Box with carved handle; **Jo Winter** Suspended box.

GMC Publications would also like to thank the editor of *Woodturning* magazine, in which earlier versions of all the projects were first published.

SUPPLIERS

3M
Bristle discs
www.3m.co.uk

Carbatec
Archer rotary tools
www.carbatec.com.au

Clear plastic supplies
Clear acrylic tubing
www.clearplasticsupplies.co.uk

Dremel
Hand-held rotary tools
www.dremel.com

DuPont UK
Corian
www.dupont.co.uk

Foredom
Hand-held rotary tools
www.foredom.net

Hermes Coated Abrasives Europe
Webrax abrasive web
www.hermes-schleifmittel.com

Jo Sonja's Artists' Colours
Acrylic paints
www.josonjas-ukshop.co.uk

Kelton Industries
Kelton hollowing tools
www.kelton.co.nz

KWH Mirka Ltd
Abranet sanding discs
www.mirka.com

Livos Australia
Kunos oil sealer
www.livos.com.au

Proxxon Tools UK
Long-neck mini grinder
www.hobbytools-direct.com

Robert Sorby
Chatter tool; Stebcentre toothed driving centre
www.robert-sorby.co.uk

Rustins
Wood bleach
www.rustins.eu

The ToolPost
Rolly Munro hollowing tools
www.toolpost.co.uk

WeCheer
Handpiece for rotary carvers
www.wecheer.com

White Diamond
Metal polishing products
www.whitediamondeu.com

Woodturner PRO
CAD program for segmented turning
woodturnerpro.com

Yandles
Timber (incl. materials used for the Ten endgrain boxes project, page 38)
www.yandles.co.uk

INDEX

To order a book, or to request a catalogue, contact:
GMC Publications Ltd
Castle Place, 166 High Street, Lewes, East Sussex
BN7 1XU, United Kingdom
Tel: +44 (0)1273 488005
www.gmcbooks.com